Samuel Bourn

On Some Select Parables of Our Savior

With an Introduction and Appendix

Samuel Bourn

On Some Select Parables of Our Savior
With an Introduction and Appendix

ISBN/EAN: 9783744761772

Printed in Europe, USA, Canada, Australia, Japan

Cover: Foto ©Thomas Meinert / pixelio.de

More available books at **www.hansebooks.com**

DISCOURSES

By SAMUEL BOURN.

VOLUME III.

DISCOURSES

BY SAMUEL BOURN.

VOLUME III.

ON SOME
SELECT PARABLES
OF
OUR SAVIOR.

IN TWO PARTS.

I. *On those contained in Matthew* xiii.
II. *On those in Luke* xv. xvi.

WITH AN
Introduction and Appendix.

THE SECOND EDITION.

Καὶ ελαλησεν αυτοις πολλα εν παραβολαις. Mat. xiii. 3.
————*Mutato nomine, de te*
Fabula narratur.————Hor. Sat. 1.

LONDON:
Printed for T. BECKET and P. A. DE HONDT,
near Surry-Street, in the Strand.
MDCCLXVIII.

CONTENTS

OF THE

THIRD VOLUME.

PART I.

On the Parables in the thirteenth Chapter of St. MATTHEW.

DISCOURSE I. II.   Page 3, 27

OF the Sower: Or, Grain dispersed upon the Surface of the Earth.

MATTHEW xiii. 1.

The same day Jesus went out of the house, and sate by the sea-side: And great multitudes were gathered together unto him; so that he went

CONTENTS.

went into a ship, and sate, and the whole multitude stood on the shore. And he spake to them many things in parables: saying, Behold, a Sower went forth to sow: &c. to the 11th.

DISCOURSE III. IV. Page 53, 75

Of the Harvest: Or, Separation of the Tares from the Wheat.

MATTHEW xiii. 24—31.

Another parable put he forth unto them, saying, The kingdom of heaven is likened unto a man which sowed good seed in his field. But while men slept, his enemy came and sowed tares amongst the wheat, and went his way. But when the blade was sprung up, and brought forth fruit, then appeared the tares also. So the servants of the housholder came and said unto him, Sir, didst thou not sow good seed in thy field? From whence then hath it tares?——He said unto them, An enemy hath done this. The servants said

unto

unto him, Wilt thou then that we go and gather them up? *But he said,* Nay; lest while ye gather up the tares, ye root up also the wheat with them. Let both grow together until the harvest: and in the time of harvest I will say to the reapers, Gather ye together first the tares, and bind them in bundles to burn them: but gather the wheat into my barn.

DISCOURSE V.   Page 101.

Of the Net which gathered of every Kind: Or, the Capture and Assortment of Fishes.

MATTHEW xiii. 47.

Again, the kingdom of heaven is like unto a net which was cast into the sea, and gathered of every kind; which, when it was full, they gathered the good into vessels, but cast the bad away.——So shall it be at the end of this world: the angels shall come forth and sever the wicked from among the just, and shall cast them into the furnace of fire:

CONTENTS.

fire: there shall be weeping and gnashing of teeth.

DISCOURSE VI.   Page 123

Of the Treasure hid in a Field: And the Pearl of great Price.

MATTHEW xiii. 44.

Again, the kingdom of heaven is like unto treasure hid in a field; which when a man hath found he hideth, and for joy thereof goeth and selleth all that he hath, and buyeth that field. Again, the kingdom of heaven is like unto a merchant-man seeking goodly pearls: who when he had found one pearl of great price, he went and sold all that he had and bought it.

DISCOURSE VII.   Page 143

Of the Grain of Mustard-seed, which became the greatest of Herbs: and the Leaven which diffused itself through the whole Mass.

MATTHEW

CONTENTS.

MATTHEW xiii. 31.

Another parable put he forth unto them, saying, The kingdom of heaven is like to a grain of mustard-seed, which a man took and sowed in his field; which indeed is the least of all seeds; but when it is grown it is the greatest amongst herbs, and becometh a tree; so that the birds of the air come and lodge in the branches thereof.——Another parable spake he unto them: The kingdom of heaven is like unto leaven, which a woman took and hid in three measures of meal till the whole was leavened.

PART II.

On the Parables in the fifteenth and sixteenth Chapters of St. LUKE.

DISCOURSE I.   Page 177

The Occasion of the following Parables.

LUKE

LUKE XV. 1, 2.

Then drew nigh to him all the publicans and sinners for to hear him. And the pharisees and scribes murmured, saying, This man receiveth sinners, and eateth with them.

DISCOURSE II.   Page 201
Of the careful Shepherd.

LUKE XV. 3.——&c.

And he spake this parable unto them, saying, What man among you having an hundred sheep, if he lose one of them, doth not leave the ninety and nine in the wilderness, and go after that which is lost until he find it? And when he hath found it, he layeth it upon his shoulders rejoicing. And when he cometh home, he calleth together his friends and neighbors, saying unto them, Rejoice with me: for I have found my sheep which was lost. I say unto you, that likewise joy shall be in heaven over one sinner that repenteth, more than over ninety and nine just persons

CONTENTS.

perſons who need no repentance. Either what woman having ten pieces of ſilver, if ſhe loſe one piece, doth not light a candle, and ſweep the houſe, and ſeek diligently till ſhe find it? And when ſhe hath found it, ſhe calleth her friends and neighbors together, ſaying, Rejoice with me, for I have found the piece which I had loſt. Likewiſe I ſay unto you, there is joy in the preſence of the angels of GOD *over one ſinner that repenteth.*

DISCOURSE III. IV. Page 229, 259

Of the penitent Rake, and his compaſſionate Father.

LUKE xv. 11.

And he ſaid, A certain man had two ſons: and the younger of them ſaid to his father, Father, give me the portion of goods that falleth to me. And he divided unto them his living. And not many days after, the younger ſon gathered all together, and took his

CONTENTS.

his journey into a far country, and there wasted his substance with riotous living. And when he had spent all, there arose a mighty famine in that land; and he began to be in want. And he went and joined himself to a citizen of that country; and he sent him into his fields to feed swine. And he would fain have filled his belly with the husks that the swine did eat: and no man gave unto him. And when he came to himself, he said, How many hired servants of my father's have bread enough and to spare, and I perish with hunger! I will arise, and go to my father, and will say unto him, Father, I have sinned against heaven, and before thee, and am no more worthy to be called thy son: make me as one of thy hired servants. And he arose, and came to his father. But when he was yet a great way off, his father saw him, and had compassion, and ran, and fell on his neck, and kissed him. And the son said unto him, Father, I have sinned against heaven, and in thy fight, and am no more worthy to be called thy fon.—*But the father faid to his fervants, Bring forth the beft robe, and put it on him, and put a ring on his hand, and fhoes on his feet: and bring hither the fatted calf, and kill it; and let us eat and be merry: for this my fon was dead, and is alive again; he was loft, and is found. And they began to be merry: Now his elder fon was in the field: and as he came and drew nigh to the houfe, he heard mufic and dancing. And he called one of the fervants, and afked what thefe things meant. And he faid unto him, Thy brother is come; and thy father hath killed the fatted calf, becaufe he hath received him fafe and found. And he was angry, and would not go in: therefore came his father out, and entreated him. And he anfwering, faid to his father, Lo, thefe many years do I ferve thee, neither tranfgreffed I any time thy commandment, and yet thou never gaveft me a kid, that I might make merry with my friends. But as foon as this thy fon was come, which hath devoured*

CONTENTS.

devoured thy living with harlots, thou hast killed for him the fatted calf. And he said unto him, Son, thou art ever with me, and all that I have is thine. It was meet that we should make merry, and be glad: for this thy brother was dead, and is alive again; and was lost, and is found.

DISCOURSE V. VI. Page 283, 309

Of the subtle Steward, or hardened Villain.

LUKE xvi. 1, &c. to 8.

And he said unto his disciples, There was a certain rich man which had a steward; and the same was accused unto him that he had wasted his goods. And he called him, and said unto him, How is it that I hear this of thee? give an account of thy stewardship; for thou mayest be no longer steward. Then the steward said within himself, What shall I do? for my lord taketh away from me the stewardship: I cannot dig; to beg I

am

CONTENTS.

am ashamed.——I am resolved what to do; that when I am put out of the stewardship, they may receive me into their houses. So he called every one of his lord's debtors unto him; and said unto the first, How much owest thou unto my lord? And he said, An hundred measures of oil. And he said unto him, Take thy bill, and sit down quickly, and write fifty. Then said he to another, And how much owest thou? And he said, An hundred measures of wheat. And he said unto him, Take thy bill, and write fourscore. And the lord commended the unjust steward, because he had done wisely.

DISCOURSE VII. VIII. Page 335, 363
Of the inhuman rich *Jew*, and his Brethren.

LUKE xvi. from 19. to the end.

There was a certain rich man, which was cloathed in purple and fine linen, and fared sumptuously every day. And there was a certain beggar named Lazarus, which was laid at his gate full of sores; and desiring

to be fed with the crumbs which fell from the rich man's table: moreover the dogs came and licked his sores. And it came to pass that the beggar died; and was carried by the angels into Abraham's bosom. The rich man also died and was buried. And in hell he lift up his eyes, being in torments, and seeth Abraham afar off, and Lazarus in his bosom. And he cried, and said, Father Abraham, have mercy on me; and send Lazarus, that he may dip the tip of his finger in water, and cool my tongue: for I am tormented in this flame. But Abraham said, Son, remember, that thou in thy life-time receivedst thy good things, and likewise Lazarus evil things: but now he is comforted, and thou art tormented. And besides all this, between us and you there is a great gulf fixed: so that they which would pass from hence to you, cannot; neither can they pass to us, that would come from thence. Then he said, I pray thee, therefore, father, that thou wouldest send him to my father's house: for I have
five

CONTENTS.

five brethren; that he may testify unto them, lest they also come into this place of torment. Abraham saith unto him, They have Moses and the prophets, let them hear them. And he said, Nay, father Abraham; but if one went unto them from the dead, they will repent. And he said unto him, If they hear not Moses and the prophets, neither will they be persuaded, though one rose from the dead.

DISCOURSE IX. Page 397
Our Savior reproves the Vanity of his Apostles.

LUKE xvii. 1—10.

Then said he unto the disciples, It is impossible but that offences will come: but wo unto him through whom they come. It were better for him that a milstone were hanged about his neck, and he cast into the sea, than that he should offend one of these little ones. Take heed to yourselves: If thy brother trespass against thee, rebuke him; and if he repent, forgive him. And if he trespass against

CONTENTS.

against thee seven times in a day, and seven times in a day turn again to thee, saying, I repent; thou shalt forgive him. And the apostles said unto the Lord, Increase our faith. And the Lord said, If ye had faith as a grain of mustard-seed, ye might say unto this sycamine-tree, Be thou plucked up by the root, and be thou planted in the sea; and it should obey you. But which of you having a servant plowing, or feeding cattle, will say unto him by and by, when he is come from the field, Go and sit down to meat? And will not rather say unto him, Make ready wherewith I may sup, and gird thyself, and serve me, till I have eaten and drunken; and afterward thou shalt eat and drink? Doth he thank that servant because he did the things that were commanded him? I trow not. So likewise ye, when ye shall have done all those things which are commanded you, say, We are unprofitable servants: we have done that which was our duty to do.

APPENDIX.   Page 421

INTRO-

INTRODUCTION.

THE fabulous or allegorical manner of conveying inftruction appears to have been held in high efteem in all ages, and generally acceptable, not only to the inferior people, but to perfons of the beft education and moft refined tafte. The original fimplicity and beauty of it are beft relifhed by thofe whofe tafte is moft natural. The properties of this fpecies of compofition have been well defcribed by fome modern writers, particularly Mr. *Dodfley*. Yet there is one point, in which I cannot avoid differing from him. For, whatever the purport of the fable may be, whether moral, prudential, political, or religious,—to prefix the application, feems to be reverfing the proper order, and placing things ὕϛερον πρότερον.—It anticipates the reader's judgment, and prevents him from exercifing his own thought and invention;—

INTRODUCTION.

tion;—takes away that agreeable surprize and strength of impression, which his own discovery of the writer's design, and skill in the execution of it, would otherwise give him; and consequently weakens if not destroys the very intended effect: yet this rule admits of exceptions, where the fable is introduced as an incidental part of a discourse.

It will be allowed, I presume, by the best judges, upon a fair examination and comparison, that our *Savior* hath far excelled all other fabulists, and carried this species of instruction to a perfection, unknown before his time, and unequalled since. The principal properties, by which his compositions are distinguished from all others of the like kind, seem to be these.

First, His actors are not the inferior creatures, but *men*.—Sometimes he leads us to draw instruction from the inferior living creatures, and the process of things in the vegetable world;—and in short, to consider all nature as a vast scene, every part of which

INTRODUCTION.

which we may study to our great advantage and improvement. But the species of mankind is a principal and distinguished part of this spectacle of nature. Here lies therefore the fullest source of instruction, in regard to morality and religion, as well as civil prudence and policy.—Our late poet indeed represents the Maker of man as saying to him at his formation,—" Go, from " the *creatures* thy instructions take," &c. But he did not mean to imply, that we cannot receive more and better instruction from the study of *human* nature, and a right attention to the various occurrences in human society. For he says elsewhere, " The proper science of mankind is man."— Undoubtedly, men themselves are the more proper actors in a scene, and speakers in a dialogue, formed for the instruction of mankind. In like manner then, as others had employed the lower creatures; our *Savior* thought fit to introduce into his scenes men only: by which, he adds to the significance, without diminishing the

INTRODUCTION.

ease and familiarity of the narration. And we may well suppose, that in some view similar to that in which we may behold the lower animals, he might consider mankind, compared to that superior and angelic order of beings, of which he frequently makes mention, and in a manner which implies his knowledge of their nature.

How greatly his compositions excel also, in concisenefs, variety, and perspicuity, will be acknowledged by a judicious and impartial critic. Scarce a single circumstance or expression can be taken away from any of them, without injuring the whole. They also comprehend the most extensive and important meaning, in the shortest compass of narration; and afford at the same time the largest scope to the judgment and reflection of the reader. Some of them comprehend no dialogue, and scarce any action, and are little more than a simple comparison, in which a resemblance is pointed out,

INTRODUCTION.

out, in some important circumstance, between things very different—between the subject unknown and to be investigated, and something very well known. In others, we may easily trace the outlines of a compleat drama:—various remarkable characters and incidents are brought together, and regularly disposed—perplexity and distress arise in the course of the action—and the conclusion discovers the design of the whole; or an application is added.—The obscurity which may be thought to lie in some of them, wholly arises from our not clearly understanding *his character*, or that of his audience, or the occasion on which he spoke:—except where the subject itself rendered some obscurity unavoidable. Yet if we consider the nature of *such* subjects, as those of a future state, an invisible world, and administration of affairs in it, and how inadequate our minds are to such conceptions; there may appear perhaps the most admirable perspicuity in his representations of these things. It may be thought, that

INTRODUCTION.

by the familiarity of his allusions and descriptions, he intended to throw off that *mysterious* grandeur and obscurity in them, by which they confound the mind, elude the search of reason, and consequently give scope only to the delusions of imagination. For where we are most in the dark, fancy is often most powerful and active, and most likely to mislead us. He therefore leads us to form ideas of the most sublime and mysterious things, from things most familiar and intelligible; and of the transactions of superior Beings, from the common prudence, justice, and humanity of men in their treatment of one another, and in their discernment and management of things subject to their use. In others of them, which were intended as an apology for himself, or confutation of his adversaries, or solution of some question, or persuasion to some duty, or prediction of some event; the main point of his design, and the propriety of the circumstances thrown in, as conducive to that end, or affording

instruction

INTRODUCTION.

instruction and entertainment coincident with it, may be easily understood, and will certainly be admired, by all who study them with attention and ingenuity.—After all, it depends as much upon the capacity and attention of the hearer or reader, as upon the structure of the fable, whether its meaning and propriety shall be understood or not. How often does it happen that a story, well told in company, appears perfectly intelligible to one part of them, yet it is misunderstood, or thought intricate and obscure, by the other. It is, for the most part, an useless attempt, if not impossible, to make things so plain, that no man can mistake them. And the aim of every good writer, is not to save his reader the trouble of thinking upon the subject, but to engage his thought and attention; that so he may make use of his own understanding and reflection, together with the assistance offered, in acquiring knowledge.

Another peculiar excellence of his parables, is the frequent introduction of *his*

INTRODUCTION.

own character into them, as the principal figure, and in views so various, important and significant:—for instance, the sower—the vine-dresser—the proprietor of an estate—the careful shepherd—the just master—the kind father—the splendid bridegroom—the potent nobleman—the heir of a kingdom—and the King upon his throne of glory judging the whole world of mankind.—A striking contrast hence arises, between the simplicity of his descriptions, and the dignity of the speaker.

Another material and distinguishing circumstance, consists in his speaking these parables, just as occasions were offered, in the ordinary course of his conversation and instruction, privately as well as publickly, to his own disciples, to the multitude, and to the pharisees and chief rulers.—An accidental question, or unexpected event appears, to have been the occasion of some of them:—for instance, that of the good *Samaritan*, when he was asked, *who is my neighbor?*——

INTRODUCTION.

neighbor?—that of *the rich man whose ground brought forth plentifully*, when he was applied to, to determine a suit concerning an estate——that of *the barren fig-tree*, when he was told of the *Galileans* whom *Pilate* had massacred—that of *a certain man who made a great supper*, when he was present at a splendid entertainment—and those of *the careful shepherd*, the *prodigal son*, the *unjust steward*, and the *inhuman rich Jew*; when a great number both of publicans and sinners, and of pharisees and scribes, happened to be present, and the latter openly murmured against him and insulted him.—It will seem very unnatural to any person, who attends to the history, to imagine that these were precomposed, from a mere human prudential foresight of such emergencies: yet on that supposition they merit high admiration. If they were not, then, what conception ought we to entertain of such a genius and wisdom, united with a goodness and power more than human?—

INTRODUCTION.

human?—and what respect do his instructions deserve?

It is hoped this preface may suffice, to bespeak the reader's serious and candid perusal of the following discourses; which are an attempt to place some of those parables in a natural, entertaining, and useful point of view.

PART I.

On the Parables in the thirteenth Chapter of St. MATTHEW.

FROM comparing the several evangelists together, we find that *these* were all spoke on the same day, and to the same audience. A vast multitude being gathered about our Savior, he went into a vessel on the side of the lake of *Capernaum*, and from thence delivered these fables to them, as they stood upon the rising shore— a very advantageous situation for being heard. When he taught another multitude from the eminence of a hill, he made *no* use of parables, but spoke in a plain didactic sententious preceptive manner: But to this multitude, it is said, "That he spoke in "parables

"parables *only*:" And they are doctrinal, characteristic, descriptive of himself, his disciples, his audience, *Christians* in general, the effects of christianity, and the future state of mankind as connected with the present. It may be impossible for us to assign the particular reasons for which he took so different methods. Only it may be alledged in general, in the words of a late excellent author and critic *, " That it is
" necessary sometimes for wise men to
" speak in parables, and with a double
" meaning — that the enemy may be a-
" mused, and they only *who have ears to*
" *hear may hear*. For we can never do
" more injury to truth, than by discovering
" too much of it on some occasions. 'Tis
" the same with understandings as with
" eyes — to such a certain size and make,
" just so much light is necessary, and no
" more. Whatever is beyond brings dark-
" ness and confusion."

* Shaftesb.

DISCOURSE I.

Of the Sower: Or, Grain dispersed upon the Surface of the Earth.

MATTHEW xiii. 1.

The same day Jesus went out of the house, and sate by the sea-side: And great multitudes were gathered together unto him; so that he went into a ship, and sate, and the whole multitude stood on the shore. And he spake to them many things in parables: saying, Behold, a Sower went forth to sow: &c. to the 11th.

OF all methods of instruction, the use of *Parables*, that is, of comparisons, allegories, and fables, seems to be the most ingenious, and most proper to exercise the thinking faculties, though not to raise the passions. It appears simple and easy to the reader or hearer, yet is very difficult to the author. A peculiar

genius

genius is requisite to convey instruction of any kind in this manner, with propriety and success. Very few masters have appeared, in the course of many ages, equal to the design. To deliver, then, the most important instructions of religion in this method, on sudden emergencies, and without premeditation, may justly be thought to surpass human invention.—Now many instances may be alledged to shew, that our Savior raised his parables and instructions from the immediate object or occasion, and with a reference to things present at the time and place; and consequently, that his discourses, in those instances, were not the effect of study and premeditation. Hence arises a particular argument for the truth of Christianity; of the validity of which the wisest men will be the most sensible. For if the parabolic manner of instruction be so difficult; if in nations abounding with men of learning and genius, none were ever able, even with the help of previous study, to speak

and

and inftruct in this manner, and with equal fimplicity and propriety as *Jefus* of *Nazareth* did; it is a natural and unavoidable queftion, *Whence had this man this wifdom?* And in refolving this important queftion, the more we attend to the meannefs and impediments of his worldly condition and education, amongft an ignorant and fuperftitious people, the more we fhall be convinced that this wifdom was fupernatural: Since notwithftanding the greateft difadvantages, he arofe, at once, from the loweft ftate of obfcurity, became a light to the world, and fhone out with the brighteft luftre of wifdom, truth and goodnefs.

It is a proof of his perfect *integrity* alfo, that inftead of addrefling himfelf to the paffions of the people, and aiming to win their applaufe or affection by pompous, pleafing or pathetic declamations, he took a method fo much the reverfe: For when, by the fame of his miracles, liftening multitudes were gathered around him, inftead of haranguing upon topics proper to move and captivate the populace; he relates to them a fable or ftory, invented for the particular time and purpofe, plain and fimple in appearance, but which had an important meaning and defign. Nor did he vouchfafe to explain the meaning publicly; fo that the foolifh and prejudiced would defpife his words, whilft the thinking and well-difpofed would difcover fomething of the intended inftruction. *Behold*, faith he, *a Sower went forth to fow: And as he fowed, fome feed fell on the wayfide, and the fowls of the air came and devoured it: Some fell on ftony places, which foon fprung up, and foon withered away, becaufe there was no depth of foil: Some fell amongft thorns, which grew up with it and choaked it: But fome fell on good ground, which grew up to maturity, and brought forth fruit, part an hundred fold, part fixty, and part thirty.*

It

It is probable, that but few would comprehend the moral design of this familiar narration; that some would receive it with contempt, and others be amused rather than instructed. He precludes all objections by only adding, *He that hath ears to hear let him hear.* The disciples themselves did not understand him, but desired an explanation; and asked him, why he spoke to the people in a manner so obscure and enigmatical? He replies, That it was on account of their stupidity and prejudices, which rendered the greater part of them either incapable of instruction, or averse to receive it in an open undisguised manner: And therefore it was necessary to veil the light of truth from their weak and distempered eyes; yet not to conceal his meaning so far, but that the impartial attentive hearer might receive the benefit of his instruction; whilst others, whose *hearts were waxed gross,* and *their ears dull of hearing,* and *their eyes closed, in seeing would not perceive, and in* hear-

hearing would not understand; that is, would remain unconvinced and diffatisfied with his difcourfe.

Many Chriftians now read or hear the parables and other inftructions of our Savior, without any notion of employing their own faculties in order to comprehend and apply what is faid. They are acquainted perhaps with his words; but as to the meaning and defign, the compafs and depth of thought, the wifdom and philofophy contained in them, they know little or nothing, nor ever think of applying their minds to fuch kind of ftudy. They only defire to be amufed with a difcourfe, to have their paffions foothed, or their fancy pleafed; not to have their underftandings informed, or to be convinced of their errors, or amended of their faults. The Gofpel is nothing but a found of words in the ears of fuch perfons: And well did *Efaias* prophefy, not only of *Jews*, but of many *Chriftians* alfo, faying, *Make the heart of this people fat, and their ears dull of hearing, and close up their eyes;* so that in seeing or hearing the instructions of our Savior, they shall not understand them, nor make any use of their thinking faculties, in order to their own conversion and amendment.

But if it is given to us to know the mysteries of the kingdom of Heaven; if we have an ear to hear, and a mind to understand; if we are able to distinguish sense from sound, and an important meaning from a pomp of words; if we are both capable and willing to be instructed, and do not think ourselves already too wise to learn the lessons which the great Teacher sent from God hath taught; let us now employ our best attention and industry in searching for the hidden treasure contained in his words; and then we shall assuredly receive some important and useful instruction.

He

He condescended himself to explain the parable to his own disciples, in the following terms.—*When any man heareth the word of the kingdom, but doth not understand it; then cometh the wicked one and catcheth away that which was sown in his heart: This is he that receiveth the seed by the way-side. But he that receiveth the seed into stony places, is the man who heareth the Gospel, and for the present receives it joyfully, but it takes no root in his heart; and as soon as any difficulty occurs, he is offended. He also that receiveth the seed among the thorns, is the man who heareth the word; but the care of this world, and the deceitfulness of riches choak it, and he becomes unfruitful. But he that receiveth the seed into the good ground, is the man who heareth the word, and understandeth it, who also beareth fruit, and bringeth forth thirty, sixty, or an hundred fold.*—— This is our *Savior*'s own explanation. But it will not enable us, without a further and close attention, to comprehend the full mean-

meaning and design of the parable, either in the whole, or in its several parts.

For he here describes, in a familiar and striking figure, his own character, that of his disciples, and that of the multitude, according to the present time and situation in which he was then speaking to them. He predicts also the operation and effect which he foresaw the Gospel would have, according to the different tempers and capacities of individual persons. In other places he describes the effect of it in different ages and nations, and foretells the opposition it would meet with, and the injuries and oppressions of which it would be the innocent occasion. But here he speaks of the neglect or disregard which would be shewn to it by many who would seem at first to give some attention to it: and foretells how ineffectual it would prove to the general instruction and reformation of mankind, even where it would meet with no direct opposition.

Let

Let us now attend, in the firſt place, to the propriety of the parabolic figure or allegory which our Savior makes uſe of. 2dly, To the general meaning and deſign of the parable. 3dly, To the ſeveral parts, or the characters which are ſeparately and diſtinctly deſcribed.

First, to the propriety of the figure or allegory.——The wiſdom of God hath perfectly adapted the earth and its inhabitants the one to the other. There is a mutual fitneſs and coherence in all the works of God. Human nature, and the ſuperficies of the earth, have a relation and ſimilitude. As the bodies of all plants and animals riſe, grow, come to maturity, and decay; the minds of men are ſubject alſo to the ſame order of nature. And as there is a variety of climates and ſoils, ſome fertile, others barren; ſuch is the variety alſo of tempers and capacities in mankind; and ſuch it was intended to be by the Maker of all things. And there is

more

more wisdom and goodness of design in this variety than we are able to conceive. It would undoubtedly appear to us, if we could fully comprehend things, not a blemish or defect, but a beauty and excellence. If any should be disposed to object, Why hath not GOD given to all men equal capacity of understanding, or equal goodness of nature?---beside the general answer, *Who art thou, O Man, that replyest against GOD? Shall the thing formed say to him who formed it, Why hast thou made me thus?* —— We might as reasonably ask, why GOD hath not made all lands and climates of the earth of equal goodness and fertility? Why in some places there is found a rich and generous soil, while others are so barren as to exclude all hope of improvement or produce? This, we need not doubt, is a just and admirable variety, though it may not always correspond to human fancy or opinion. The most rugged and desolate parts of the earth have their beauty and use in the eye of their

Ma-

Maker; and so have the most savage nations, the most uncultivated part of mankind: All fill up their proper place in the wide creation, and every variety serves to display the manifold wisdom of GOD.

But as it is evidently the intention of divine Providence, that the *soil of the earth* should be cultivated, and produce plenty of fruits for the support of mankind; and as he hath given us, to this very end, the grain that is to be sown upon it; so it is equally, or much more agreeable to his intention, that *human nature* should be cultivated, and the minds of men be made productive of the noble harvest of wisdom and virtue: And to this very end, he hath given to men those instructions of true religion, which when they meet with a proper capacity and temper to receive them, will yield a valuable increase, like pure grain sown upon fertile land. But it follows at the same time, that the Gospel itself will take effect in the world only in proportion to men's natural capacity and difpofition to receive it. And as vaft tracts of the earth remain to this day barren or uncultivated, notwithftanding all the means of culture which providence hath afforded; fo notwithftanding the publication of the Gofpel, many nations remain uninftructed; and in the moft improved Chriftian nations, the effect is, and always will be, various, according to the difference of particular perfons. Some will not underftand it, and it will never make the leaft impreffion upon their minds. Others will receive it with a fudden approbation and pleafure, but not lafting. Others will fuffer worldly cares and paffions to grow up with it and choke it. While fome will receive it with judgment and underftanding; and being convinced of its truth, will make it, from a principle of natural honefty, the fpecial rule of their conduct, and ground of their fatisfaction and hope.

When the great *Sower*, our *Savior* himself, *went forth to sow*, i. e. to scatter abroad the instructions of the Gospel among the people; some were inclined, others averse to hear him: Some were capable, others incapable of understanding him: Some heard him with a good, some with an evil intention, and others with a mere undesigning curiosity: Many received no benefit from his instructions, either thro' stupidity, or levity, or worldliness of temper: While some received the word with understanding and honesty of heart, and made a right improvement of it.

In order to express these various effects, which he perfectly understood and foresaw, he compares *human nature* to the *surface of the earth*, and the different *minds and tempers* of men to the different *kinds of soil:* He describes *himself* in the character of the *Sower*, and the *Gospel* he taught in the figure of *Grain* scattered abroad upon the earth: Wisdom and virtue are the
Har-

Harvest it was intended to produce: But no harvest is to be expected from impenetrable and barren ground, or that is overrun with thorns and briars; but only from *fertile* land, and in proportion to the strength and goodness of the soil.

This leads us, in the second place, to the general meaning and design of the parable.——In order to make improvement in any business, art or science, two qualifications are requisite in conjunction; namely, *capacity* and *attention*. If either of them is wanting, the other alone will not suffice. A habit of attention is an excellent qualification, but will answer no purpose if there be not a sufficient capacity. It is therefore highly advantageous to consider the limits which God hath assigned to the human understanding; lest we should vainly attempt to penetrate beyond our reach, or to sound unfathomable depths. It has been the vanity and folly of Christians to give too much attention to what have been called the mysteries of religion; and instead of learning and practising that which is revealed, to employ themselves and trouble others about that which is unrevealed and cannot be understood. The unhappy consequence of which hath been, that whilst they were so busy about things above their capacity, they remained ignorant of, or greatly neglected, things most intelligible and conducive to virtue. All that is important and useful in the doctrines of religion is at the same time level to human capacity: We may gain the knowledge of it, if we will but apply our minds to it. But as on the one hand, a busy attention to things above our understandings will be of no advantage; so on the other, a mere capacity of comprehending any subject will be of no use without honest attention. This is most remarkably true in regard to religion: For it is to this subject that an impartial and close attention is most of all requisite; and vanity, prejudice, pride, passion, and other impediments most frequently intervene, stop the free course of inquiry, and bar the entrance of truth into the mind.———It must be allowed of the holy Scriptures in general, and of our *Savior's* parables in particular, that there is some difficulty and obscurity in them. For GOD hath not left the science of religion and the truths of christianity exposed to the idle and careless, the prejudiced and dishonest part of mankind. On the contrary, the knowledge of true religion, like that of any other subject of importance, cannot be obtained without previous application: And the improvement will be in proportion to the sincere and assiduous endeavours that are used in obtaining it. There are undoubtedly different degrees of capacity in mankind with regard to religion, as well as other subjects. Some are far more able than others to discern what seems obscure, to determine what hath been thought doubtful, to distinguish things different, to form clear and just sentiments, and to act upon solid principles and extensive views: And greater improvements may be made by such greater abilities: From him *that hath ten talents*, a proportionate increase may be expected. But every man has a capacity sufficient for his own salvation: And the righteous Governor of the world will never condemn any man for not having what is not given to him, but for not improving what was given. And therefore, an honest and diligent application is the main thing wanting to every man's own salvation: tho' still men's respective improvements in virtue and religion will hold a proportion to their different capacity, as well as honesty and industry. Those will make the best improvements of the Gospel who receive it, and understand it, and retain it in honest and good hearts: And the produce will be in proportion to the natural understanding, sincerity, constancy, and diligence of them that receive it.

BUT

But it is in vain that the Sower scatters abroad the seed, if there be not a proper soil to receive it. The purity and richness of the grain cannot supply for the natural poverty of the land. For if it is either so hard and beaten, that the grain cannot enter it at all, or so shallow of soil that it can take no root, or so full of thorns and weeds, that they will out-grow and choke it; there can be no harvest. A right disposition of the soil is as necessary as the sowing of the grain. So in moral and spiritual things, there must be a right disposition of mind, a sensibility of heart, a habit of attention, a freedom from passion and prejudice, a design to learn and to improve; without which, no doctrines, no arguments, no persuasions will have any good and lasting effect. They will either make no impression at all, or raise but a slight and transient emotion, or be over-born and suppressed by contrary cares and passions. Persons of the best natural capacity and temper will make the best use of religious instructions; according to the sentiment of the wise King, *A wise man will hear and will increase knowledge, and a man of understanding will attain unto wise counsels. Give instruction to a wise man, and he will be yet wiser: Teach a just man, and he will increase in learning.* And again, *If thou wilt incline thine ear unto wisdom, and apply thy heart to understanding: If thou seekest for it as silver, and searchest for it as for hidden treasure; then shalt thou understand the fear of the Lord, and find the knowledge of GOD.*——It is wisdom alone which gains wisdom, and goodness alone which improves in goodness. If there is no natural stock of sense and honesty for the Gospel to be grafted upon, it will produce nothing. The less understanding a man is possessed of already, he is the less capable of gaining more: And where there is no natural sense and knowledge, none can ever be attained. In like manner, the less honesty any person is indued with, he is so much the less capable of increasing in virtue: And if we could suppose a person destitute of all moral sense and goodness, none could ever be produced in him, by any art or application: The best instructions and most powerful persuasions would have no more effect, than grain thrown away upon the *beaten road* or *impenetrable rock*. It is a vain thing to teach them that will not be taught, or argue with them who have no judgment, or persuade them to any thing good who have no disposition to it. The aptitude of the learner must concur with the ability of the teacher. Where the mind is barred by any impediment against conviction, the clearest arguments cannot convince: And whether the temper be obstinate and insensible, or light and inconstant, or possessed by worldly cares and passions; in any of these cases, it will either obstruct the entrance at first, or at last destroy the effect, of the most excellent instructions and weightiest considerations that can be offered in any manner whatsoever. But where the instrucstructions of wisdom meet with a natural capacity and sensibility of mind, and the persuasions to virtue with a natural honesty and good disposition of heart; there they will take effect, and be *as good seed sown upon good ground:* They will spring up and come to maturity; and the increase will be in due proportion, *thirty, sixty, or a hundred fold.*—Our *Savior* sums up all that hath been said in one proverbial expression—*To him that hath shall be given: But from him that hath not shall be taken away even that which he seemeth to have.*

Thus far we have considered the general spirit and purpose of this excellent parable. We shall proceed in the next place to take into consideration the several parts of it.—In the mean time, may God give us all a right understanding and disposition to receive the truths of religion, through *Jesus Christ* our Lord.

DISCOURSE II.

Of the Sower: Or, Grain difperfed upon the Surface of the Earth.

MATTHEW xiii. 18, to 24.

Hear ye therefore the parable of the Sower. When any one heareth the word of the kingdom and understandeth it not, then cometh the wicked one, and catcheth away that which was sown in his heart: This is he which receiveth seed by the way-side. But he that receiveth the seed into stony places, the same is he that heareth the word, and anon with joy receiveth it: Yet hath he not root in himself, but dureth for a while: for when tribulation or persecution ariseth because of the word, by and by he is offended. He also that received seed among the thorns, is he that heareth the word, and the care of this world, and the deceitfulness of riches choke the word, and he becometh unfruitful. But he that received seed into the good ground,

ground, is he that heareth the word, and understandeth it, which also beareth fruit, and bringeth forth, some an hundred fold, some sixty, some thirty.

OUR *Savior* here stiles the Gospel *the word of the kingdom.* Let us consider the meaning of this phrase, lest we should be found in the number of those *who bear the word of the kingdom, but understand it not.*—It is the life to come, or that future state or world to which good men shall be raised after death, that is here especially and directly meant, by *the kingdom.* This is frequently stiled by our Savior, *his kingdom*; and likewise the *kingdom of GOD,* and *of Heaven*; and by his Apostles, *the everlasting kingdom of our Lord and Savior.* The *word* of the kingdom, then, is that *doctrine* which teaches men to believe, expect, and prepare for that life and world which are to come. To *preach* the Gospel or the word of the kingdom, is to persuade men to repentance and virtue by the motives

tives of the world to come, and as the necessary qualifications for partaking of the kingdom and glory of our Savior. Therefore, when men hear the doctrine of our Savior and his Apostles concerning the future state of immortality, and the requisite qualifications for attaining it; they then hear *the word of the kingdom*.

Now the *hearers* of this word are distinguished into four different classes, which follow each other in a regular gradation. The *first* are those on whom it makes no impression: The *second*, where it makes a very slight and transient one: The *third*, where it makes a stronger and more lasting, but which, nevertheless, is in time overpowered: And the *fourth*, where it has a permanent influence, and produces its proper effect.—We shall treat of these in their due order.

The *first* are thus described. *When any man heareth the word of the kingdom, and under-*

derstandeth it not, then cometh the wicked one and catcheth away that which is sown in his heart. Here are the stupid and insensible part of mankind, whose minds are callous and impenetrable, like the hard beaten path. How clear and intelligible soever the instructions of religion are, they do not understand them: How weighty and important soever the arguments, they do not regard them. They bestow not the least attention upon any thing of that nature; but are absolutely careless and indifferent. Religion and the doctrine of a world to come is a subject which seems foreign to them, and about which they have no concern: They will not allow themselves a moment's reflection upon it; and therefore have no conception of its meaning and importance. When such men hear the word of the kingdom, they understand it not: they never think of it, or comprehend it in their minds: It gains no entrance into their hearts; but is to them a *word without a meaning :* And therefore,

fore, like the *grain which falls upon the beaten path, and which the birds of the air come and devour,* so it falls upon the surface of their minds, and *the wicked one cometh and catcheth it away: i. e.* the most trivial object or occasion, the most vain and volatile fancy, the most foolish or wicked prejudice, or the slightest suggestion of an evil companion, is sufficient to draw off their attention, and entirely exclude the gospel from their hearts. Our Savior does not mean a total want of capacity to understand it, (which could not be the fault of any, and is the infelicity of very few) but that stupid or scornful want of attention, which will as effectually hinder men from understanding it, and being made sensible of its truth, excellence and importance, as a want of natural capacity. If men either consider the gospel as a subject in which themselves are not interested; or expect that religion will spring up in their minds without any care or study of their own; they never will understand it. They might

might as well have been born idiots, or be entirely deprived of their reason, as to any right knowledge, or good purpose of religion. These are the most incurable of mankind: no remedy will operate; instruction will take no hold of their minds; argument or persuasion will make no impression upon their hearts; truth (powerful as it is) can never overcome such invincible negligence and stupidity.

The *second* class or character of men contains *those, who hear the word, and for the present with joy receive it:* but as soon as any difficulty arises, they are disgusted, and all their religion *withers and dies away.* These are the shallow, light, superficial minds, in which the gospel can take no root, because there is *no depth of soil.* The truths of religion have a natural dignity in them, virtue and goodness an attractive charm, and the prospect of immortality is sublime and delightful: and therefore the gospel may for a while entertain and

and pleafe fuch perfons. And fo long as their curiofity is gratifyed or imagination amufed; they will feem to be very religious, and the word fown in their hearts will feem to fpring up with a furprizing quicknefs of growth. So long as religion requires nothing from them that is difficult, nor oppofes their opinions or inclinations, they efteem and love it, and appear full of affection for it. But notwithftanding all this, they do not mean to fuffer any thing for righteoufnefs fake, or enter into the kingdom of heaven through any kind of tribulation. As far as religion is a pleafure, or coincides with their temporal views, they value it: but have no notion of undergoing ftudy, labour, or expence for the fake of it. The found of divine grace and eternal falvation is agreeable to them, and they appear to receive the tidings with a joyful welcome: but ftill they mean to be faved in their own way; and to gain the kingdom of heaven without lofing any thing upon earth. Not one point of worldly intereſt or pleaſure will they ſacrifice to it. As ſoon as ever the word of the kingdom attacks their pride, or any of their favorite opinions or inclinations, or puts them to any inconvenience, they are offended: they quarrel with the goſpel, and all the good effect of it is deſtroyed. The ſame thing happens to ſome perſons through mere levity, and becauſe they have no conſtancy or reſolution: for a while they ſeem to apply themſelves with wonderful alacrity to the ſtudy and practice of religion: but their ardor ſoon abates, and their attention becomes wholly diverted to ſomething elſe; which they catch at and perſue for a while, with juſt the ſame ſpirit and warmth as they had before applied to religion. In a word, they are always for ſomething new: and the goſpel itſelf pleaſes them no longer than it has the appearance of novelty.

In this claſs we may place thoſe alſo, who

who receive the gospel with some degree of knowledge and esteem, and are really desirous of living according to it: but thro' a mere impotence of mind, fail of discharging the duties they are inclined to perform, and yield to the temptations which they wish to overcome. They approve of religion and every thing it teaches and requires: but have not strength and steadiness sufficient to put in practice what their own best judgment and disposition clearly and strongly recommend to them. Here is indeed a promising appearance; but alas! nothing comes to maturity: all withers away in the *scorching season*, because there is no depth of soil.

THE *third* class or character comprehends *those, who hear the word; but the cares of this world, and the deceitfulness of riches choke it, and they become unfruitful.* These men are very capable of understanding the gospel, and of attending to their own interest and happiness. The doctrine of a world to come, the importance of being faved from eternal deftruction, and of obtaining, thro' the mercy and favour of GOD, an eternal life, and the abfolute neceffity of repentance and virtue in order to falvation, ftrike their confciences with a ftrong conviction: they underftand and feel fomething of the truth and weight of thofe things: they are not fo ftupid as to make a jeft of religion, or treat the gofpel with contempt, or to be wholly unconcerned about a world to come, and indifferent to their own falvation. Nor are their minds fo light and fhallow, as to be incapable of retaining things of moment, or of adhering to what they are convinced is neceffary to their future fafety and happinefs. But this world hath too much hold of them: and when their temporal interefts interfere with their eternal, they neglect the latter for the fake of the former: The love of riches and worldly poffeffions infinuates itfelf into their hearts, and captivates their affections Hence they would willingly

lingly serve both God and Mammon: And though they are really desirous of obtaining the glorious rewards of an eternal kingdom; yet there are certain possessions and advantages in the kingdoms of this world, which they are still more desirous of acquiring and preserving, and which they cannot find in their hearts to neglect for the sake of the kingdom of heaven. The gospel enters indeed into their minds, takes root, and springs up. They are not so insensible as to think another world a trifling subject, and their own salvation a matter of no moment, nor are they void of some concern about it: But cares and concerns of another kind intervene: worldly desires and passions spring up at the same time, grow luxuriantly, spread their baneful influence, and destroy the rising seeds of virtue and religion.

The *fourth* and last rank or character is of *those, who hear the word and understand it, and keep it also in honest and good hearts:*

hearts: Here alone it grows up to maturity; and the increase or harvest is in proportion to the respective degrees of understanding and probity, in *some an hundred fold, some sixty, some thirty.*---Now in considering the effect of the gospel on the minds of such men, we may observe both its gradual operation and various effect, as both are figured to us in the text. Its gradual operation is described by the process of the grain; which must first be sown, then take root, and spring up, and at length come to maturity. This gradual and imperceptible process our Savior represents more particularly in another parable. *So is the kingdom of God, as if a man should cast seed into the ground, and should sleep, and rise for a succession of days, and the seed should spring and grow up he knoweth not how. For the earth bringeth forth of herself, first the blade, then the ear, after that the full corn in the ear.*——This plainly serves to expose the folly of those Christians who pretend to instantaneous conversions, to sudden

sudden impressions and sensible operations of God's holy Spirit upon their minds; by which they are changed (as they pretend) all at once---are born again and become new creatures in an instant, as it were by an unaccountable trick of some invisible agent.---How far such sudden and total conversions are possible, it is not necessary to determine. God may work miracles in the moral as well as the natural world, whenever his wisdom sees fit. But we may affirm with the utmost certainty, that such instances (if there be any) are different from the usual course and operation of the gospel upon men's hearts. And had our Savior intended to describe such conversions as these; he could hardly have made choice of a more improper comparison than that of grain, sown, springing up, and coming to maturity: which we all know is a work of a flow and gradual nature: whereas such instantaneous conversions would be as if seed-time and harvest came both at once; and the grain was no sooner sown,

sown, but it started up miraculously into a full and ripe ear. It is in the power of God undoubtedly to do miracles of this kind, and to confound spring and autumn, seed-time and harvest together. But they would be so many exceptions to that just order and beautiful process of nature which his wisdom hath established. And our Savior in this parable represents the gospel as operating upon men's minds wholly in a natural, and not at all in a supernatural manner. Otherwise, the beaten path, or the stony places, or the land overrun with thorns, might have produced a harvest, as well as the best of soils; and there would be no need of understanding, or attention, or care, or constancy, or any kind of endeavours; since the whole is to be done by the irresistible or efficacious operation of the Spirit of God. Nor would the quantity of the harvest depend in the least on the nature of the soil; but the increase might be an hundred fold in one place as well as in another.--Hence we may further

further obferve the great abfurdity of thofe, who fay, "That the wickedeft of men are the fitteft to come to Chrift—that the more fins they bring with them, the welcomer they fhall be---that the more corrupt their nature is, the more likely to become fubjects of grace and veffels of mercy elected to eternal falvation--- and that the lefs moral honefty men have, the better qualified to be faved by faith, and juftified by Chrift's imputed righteoufnefs."---Such fayings would be too abfurd to be repeated, had not fome men affirmed them with great earneftnefs and apparent zeal for religion. But every man that hath *ears to hear*, and confiders this parable of our Saviour with the leaft degree of underftanding and attention, will plainly perceive that he reprefents perfons of natural good fenfe and honefty of heart, as beft qualified to receive the faith and produce the fruits of the gofpel; and that thofe fruits will be greater or lefs in proportion to the feveral degrees of underftanding, standing, attention, and honesty, with which men hear and receive the word of the kingdom.

The gospel reveals to us the intentions of the Almighty Maker and Governor of the world towards mankind, agreeable to that perfect goodness, justice and mercy, which the light of nature itself teaches us to ascribe to him; intentions relating, not to *this* life, but to *another*. It contains the doctrine of a life to come and world everlasting, and of repentance and virtue as the means of our obtaining that life and world, supernaturally confirmed by the resurrection of our Saviour from the dead, who was the teacher and example of all virtue, and of the resurrection of all good men to life, honour, and immortality.--- Now *this word of the kingdom of heaven*, or this doctrine of an eternal life and world to come, and of repentance and virtue as the indispensible conditions of obtaining it, may be totally disregarded, or lightly esteemed,

esteemed, or postponed to worldly views and interests, by the stupid, the vain, or the worldly-minded: but whenever it meets with persons of a sensible, candid, attentive, and considerate disposition, of a free and firm temper of mind; it never fails to strike an impression and produce a lasting effect.

The idea of a world to come, and an immortal life to commence after death, is so vast and sublime, that the more men attend it, the more it will affect them. When this unbounded prospect first enters into an attentive and well-disposed mind, it astonishes and captivates it, fills its utmost capacity, raises the highest desires and hopes; every other passion is subdued; every other view swallowed up. But if it be the imagination alone that is amused and set at work, the idea will be effaced, the impression will wear out: reason and reflection must concur to fix this view, and establish this faith in the heart. In like

like manner, the indifpenfible obligations of repentance and virtue ftrike and convince the confcience of every attentive mind: but refolution muft follow conviction, in order to produce a lafting temper and habit. When the mind is thus prepared and qualified by reafon, reflexion, and refolution; the word of the kingdom takes root, grows up to maturity, and produces the noble fruits of wifdom and virtue in the conduct of life.

Some regard the doctrine of another world as if it were a fubject of mere fpeculation and idle curiofity, a popular report, a vulgar tale, the common found of the pulpit, a fubject diftant, foreign, impertinent, uninterefting to them. Not fo the fober and thoughtful inquirer: He knows (as every thinking perfon muft know) that nothing can be more interefting in its own nature, or more directly and intimately concern himfelf. He takes the fubject, therefore, into his moft
attentive,

attentive, cool, and sedate consideration: He retires within himself: willing to know the truth, and to form the principles and plan of his future conduct upon a solid foundation: he reasons, reflects, examines, repeats, resolves, and finally puts in execution his own best thoughts and mature resolutions. He is first of all convinced beyond all doubt, that there is a GOD, whose wisdom and power made and ordered all things, produced all the revolutions of past ages, and continually operate in all the present changes of apparent nature; forming the bodies and souls of men for the present life, removing one generation from the face of the earth, and raising up another to succeed them. He is soon convinced that the same word and power which are continually raising human souls to the possession of this life, are equally able to raise the departing spirits of men, and put them in possession of a superior and eternal life. He is desirous above all things to know a truth of such

infinite

infinite importance, and to be aſſured that it is *the actual intention of God* to raiſe mankind from the dead to another life. To this end, when he hears the word of the kingdom, he gives the utmoſt attention to it: He ſtudies and examines *the Chriſtian revelation* which pretends to *aſſure* him of this divine intention: And there he finds the judicial character of the Deity and his paternal goodneſs to mankind diſplayed in ſo lively colours, and the grand event of the reſurrection to another life declared, with ſuch marks of a divine commiſſion, and confirmed by ſuch kind of proof, in the *actual reſurrection* of our Saviour, as yields ample conviction and ſatisfaction to his mind. Having then received the goſpel, or the doctrine of a life to come, upon as full evidence as it is reaſonable in men to expect—here he fixes—his mind reſts ſatisfied—his heart is eſtabliſhed;—of this hope and confidence he never is aſhamed—this faith he holds faſt without wavering—on this ſolid baſis he builds the
ſuperſtructure

superstructure of his whole life.—This belief and view of eternal things secretly directs him in all his actions;—it is interwoven into the habit and frame of his mind, forms his manner of thinking and acting, and has an equal influence over his secret intentions and public actions—it brings him to that sincere and lasting repentance which never is repented of—excites him to every moral duty—cherishes every virtue in his heart—becomes apparent, not so much in an outward profession as in the actions of a sober, just, and beneficent life—is the guide of his whole conduct, the ground of his best hopes, and the comfort of his last moments.—This is the character of a true Christian, of him *who heareth the word of the kingdom and understandeth it, who also retaineth it in an honest and good heart, and bringeth forth fruit* to perfection.

YET among those who receive the gospel, and bring forth the fruit of it to maturity,

turity, there will be a great difference. For in some the increase will be in a far greater proportion than in others. The minds of some men are, as it were, of *a finer mould,* their understandings more clear, their tempers more firm, their good affections more vigorous, their love of virtue and hope of immortality more intense and fixed: In these the harvest will be so much the richer and more abundant: As in lands fit for the grain which is sown upon them the increase will be various: some will produce no more than thirty; while others will bring forth sixty or a hundred fold.

Now, if there is any distinction of good and evil, any virtue or praise in a Christian conduct, any difference between life and death, any importance in an eternal world, any peace and joy in the hope of a glorious immortality; let us gratefully and cordially receive *the word of the kingdom.* It is the doctrine of a world to come, the assurance of our resurrection from death to an immortal life, *the promife which God who cannot lie hath made*, the purpofe which *lay hid* in the divine counfels *from the foundation of the world*, but which is now manifefted and *afcertained* to us by the refurrection of our Lord Jesus Christ. Let this word dwell in us richly, and bring forth the fruits of righteoufnefs, peace, and joy in believing. Let not a carelefs infenfibility, or a wavering impotence and irrefolution, or the cares and delufions of the world exclude it from our hearts, or deftroy the noble effects it ought to produce. If it was worthy of a revelation from heaven; how much more of all attention and acceptance from men?—Where it is duly received, it rectifies the underftanding, enlarges the mind, amends the heart, and reforms the manners: It infpires virtue, courage, and hope in every period of life, and at the approach of death. Let us difpofe our hearts to the reception of it with fimplicity and fincerity: Let it be the fubject of our inmoft reflexions and moſt earneſt application. They that deſpiſe it, deſpiſe the word, not of *man*, but of *God*. They that *hate* this word of *life, love death,* and ſeek deſtruction.

Now, that we may ſo receive, underſtand, and improve *the word of the kingdom of heaven*, that we may become *wiſe unto ſalvation*, and our end may be everlaſting life, God of his infinite mercy grant thro' *Jeſus Chriſt* our Lord.

DISCOURSE III.

Of the Harveſt: Or, Separation of the Tares from the Wheat.

MATTHEW xiii. 24—31.

Another parable put he forth unto them, saying, The kingdom of heaven is likened unto a man which sowed good seed in his field. But while men slept, his enemy came and sowed tares amongst the wheat, and went his way. But when the blade was sprung up, and brought forth fruit, then appeared the tares also. So the servants of the housholder came and said unto him, Sir, didst thou not sow good seed in thy field? From whence then hath it tares?——He said unto them, An enemy hath done this. The servants said unto him, Wilt thou then that we go and gather them up? But he said, Nay; lest while ye gather up the tares, ye root up also the wheat with them. Let both grow together until the harvest: and in the time of harvest I will say to the reapers, Gather ye together first the tares, and bind them in bundles to burn them: but gather the wheat into my barn.

IN those natural and familiar images by which our Savior intended to inform the understandings of his disciples, and raise their minds to the knowledge of sublime truths, we may observe a beautiful variety. Each parable hath its proper scope; and was intended to represent, either the moral government of GOD, or the future state of mankind, or the purpose of our Savior's coming, or the effects of the gospel in the world, in some particular view. In the foregoing parable of the sower, he describes the different effects of the gospel according to the different dispositions and capacities of particular persons. In this of the tares intersperfed among the wheat, the view is different and of larger extent: the ideas are great and sublime: but the grandeur of them is veiled by the simplicity

simplicity of the images made use of; by which he purposely threw a shade over his meaning, lest the minds of his disciples should be astonished and confounded, rather than instructed.

We shall in the first place take a general view of the parable. Secondly, consider the several parts of it. And thirdly, attend to the principal point of the whole.

I. We are to take a general view of it.--- The world is the *scene* he describes: *Himself* the *principal character* or important personage introduced: Christians of all ages the *inferior characters:* Human life the *plot:* the future judgment the *unravelment* and conclusion. In this prospect then are comprehended the wide field of the world--- the Son of man in his human state laboring to cultivate it—the species of true and false Christians that would arise in it— and the view terminates in *the same Son of man* in his exalted state, as LORD of the world,

world, and sovereign disposer of its various produce. He surveys the whole earth, observes the state of human nature and the moral differences of mankind; foretells the effect of the gospel, the corruption of his church, and the temper and spirit of Christians in future ages; then extends his view forward to the final separation of good and evil men, the destruction of the one, and the preservation of the other; and *prefigures himself*, executing judgment on mankind, conducting the grand revolution of the world, issuing out orders to his ministers and servants, directing the most important affairs of *his kingdom*, reforming the whole order and state of it to perfection, abolishing all disorders and evils, destroying the authors of them, and promoting to honor and happiness all his faithful and obedient subjects. The moral government of God, the final execution of divine justice, and the dominion and authority of our Savior, as administring the justice of God to mankind, and conducting the process

Separation of the Tares from the Wheat. 59

cefs of things in a future ftate, by his own immediate direction, are the important fubjects here prefented to us. And the following extenfive propofitions will appear to be contained in his meaning and defigns—that the world produces good and bad men promifcuoufly, as the earth brings forth both weeds and ufeful plants—that his defign in fowing the good feed in it, was to raife up virtuous and good men. But that notwithftanding the publication and reception of the gofpel, numbers of hypocritical and wicked men would fpring up, (even within the inclofure of the Chriftian church) and would be found intermingled with genuine Chriftians; in like manner as good and bad men are mixed together in all other parts of the world—that the fpirit of the devil, the fpirit of pride and ambition, hypocrify and tyranny, would enter *the field* of the church, in time of general darknefs and ignorance, and propagate *antichriftians*, or falfe profeffors of Chriftianity;—that fome men would be
forward

forward in affuming to themfelves a capacity of diftinguifhing, and a right of judging, between true and falfe Chriftians, and of condemning and extirpating the latter.—But that the true fervants of CHRIST would confult their LORD's will in this important affair; and would forbear affuming fuch judgment to themfelves;—that he himfelf is the only judge of the hearts of men, and will in due time execute that office;—that this life is not the proper feafon for judgment;—but that there is a time appointed in the conftitution of univerfal nature, when a difcriminative judgment fhall be paffed, and final feparation made, between good and evil men;—that then the latter fhall be extirpated out of the creation, or deftroyed totally and eternally, as *tares* are *caft into the fire* in order to be entirely confumed: And the former fhall be preferved in fafety, and raifed to honor and happinefs.—The principal point of the parable is the fovereign power and authority of our LORD, as ordering the procefs and execution

cution of the final judgment. *So shall it be in the end of the world* (or as it might be rendered, *the conclusion of the age*, or *of this life*.) *The Son of man will send forth his angels; and they*, by his command and direction, *shall collect together all things that offend, and them that do iniquity, and shall throw them into the furnace of fire* prepared for their destruction.—Torment and lamentation will attend the dreadful period.—Then the state of mankind being thorowly purged and reformed, *the righteous shall shine forth as the sun in the kingdom of their Father, that kingdom which was prepared for them from the foundation of the world.*

LET us now proceed to consider, in the *second* place, the *several parts* of this parable; which not only contribute to the structure and propriety of the whole, but contain in each an important meaning and instruction.——Our Savior had represented in the preceding parable of the sower, the different tempers and capacities of men, by the

the *different kind of soil* upon the surface of the earth, the beaten, the shallow, the thorny, and the good ground. In this, he changes the figure; and represents the different characters of men by the *different produce of the same soil*, as consisting of good and valuable grain intermingled with useless or noxious weeds. The world produces mankind according to the course of nature: But care and culture are requisite to produce wise and good men; without which mankind themselves may become like those useless or pernicious plants which are not fit to be preserved but destroyed. Our Savior came to cultivate the field of the world, and to raise a valuable harvest of virtuous and good men in it. This and no other is the proper design and effect of his gospel: Yet it is certain from experience, that the Christian part of the world, as well as other parts, has been grievously overrun by persons of a very different character. Whence came this to pass?—*Did not our Savior sow good seed in his field?*

Unquestionably

Separation of the Tares from the Wheat.

Unqueftionably he did. But *whence then hath it the tares?*—Is the wickednefs of pretended Chriftians to be charged upon our Savior and his gofpel?—So fome infidels infinuate; and are continually urging the corruptions of the Chriftian world as an objection to Chriftianity itfelf. But he here exprefsly difowns it. For when his fervants are reprefented as coming to him and faying, *Sir, didft thou not fow good feed in thy field? whence then hath it the tares?—* His anfwer is, *An enemy hath done this:* an enemy to Chriftianity. There is a certain power and malice in the world which is continually working in oppofition to the influence of the gofpel, and endeavoring by fraud or force to ftifle and fupprefs it, or to fubftitute fomething elfe in the ftead of it. For not only the heathen and Mahometan powers, but popery and all ecclefiaftical tyranny, under whatfoever names they are erected, are enemies to Chriftianity: they are *the devil,* who *fowed tares in the field of the world.* For we may obferve, that

what

what is in the parable ſtiled *an enemy*, or as it is in the original, *a man that is an enemy*, is in the explanation ſtiled *the devil*. Every power which tends to ſubvert true religion, to deſtroy the happineſs or hinder the ſalvation of mankind, is in ſcripture-language *the devil*.—The wickedneſs of the Chriſtian world then is not to be charged upon the goſpel, but upon *that enemy* to it, that diabolic power and policy, which is continually operating, tho' perhaps under Chriſtian names and titles, yet in real hatred and oppoſition to Chriſtianity.

There is nothing our Savior more frequently intimates than the *ill ſucceſs* which he foreknew the goſpel would meet with: plainly declaring, that it would not be effectual to reform the world; and prophetically deſcribing its real progreſſion, together with the obſtructions it hath met with, the oppoſition which hath been made to it, and the negligence, corruption, and wickedneſs

ness of the hearers and pretended believers of it. In this parable especially, he foretells, that, tho' many sincere and good men would be produced in the world, by means of the gospel, yet they would always be mixed with persons of an opposite character; who, notwithstanding any appearance of Christianity they might assume, would have no more of the probity and virtue of real Christians in them, than the rankest weeds have of the goodness and value of pure grain; whom he therefore fitly compares to *tares* growing among the *wheat* which himself had sown in the field of the world.

'Tis universally allowed, that there are true and false, sound and unsound professors of Christianity. And in this view it might be thought by some a reasonable and useful institution, if our LORD had ordained a succession of men, to be governors and judges in his church, and invested them with a power of examining into men's principles

ciples and profeſſions, of trying the ſoundneſs of their faith, of ſeparating counterfeit from genuine Chriſtians, and of *excommunicating*, and even *extirpating* all depraved, corrupt and heretical perſons. And there have been in all ages, many Chriſtians ready to look upon themſelves as excellently qualifyed for ſuch an office. Not long ſince, it was the prevailing ſentiment of Chriſtians in general, that ſuch a power is, or ought to be lodged ſome-where or other: But they were never agreed where: whether in the biſhops of Rome, or in general councils, or in Chriſtian princes and ſtates. But ſuch a coercive power they ſeemed to think neceſſary to the very preſervation of the church of CHRIST, and the ſupport of true religion. Hence proceeded a ſpirit in all parties of judging the faith and conſcience of their fellow-Chriſtians, of cenſuring with much bitterneſs the religious principles and profeſſions of all who differed from themſelves, and of condemning thoſe who were thought

to

to hold pernicious errors, or to support an erroneous worship. Hence, many in their blind zeal have been forward to *extirpate*, and even *consume in the fire*, these *supposed tares* growing in the field of the Christian church: thinking it highly injurious to religion, *to let them grow together with the wheat, until the harvest*. This has in fact been the crying grievance of the Christian church, the cause of horrible injustice and cruelty; whilst the best Christians were often persecuted and destroyed instead of the worst; the wheat eradicated and committed to the flames, along with, or instead of the tares. What else could be expected; when blind and presumptuous mortals arrogated to themselves that jurisdiction over the faith and conscience of mankind, which the Father Almighty hath committed to CHRIST alone, the only qualified and worthy judge?—For when the servants are represented as enquiring further, *Wilt thou then that we go and gather up the tares?* He replied, *No: lest while ye gather up the* tares ye root up also the wheat with them. Let both grow together until the harvest.— From which it may be inferred, that instead of giving, he hath denyed to his servants all power of separating true Christians from false, and of extirpating the latter: that he did not think any of them qualified for such an office; but hath expressly reserved all such judicial procedure to himself and to the final judgment. *Let both grow together until the harvest: and in the time of harvest, I will say to the reapers, Gather ye together, first the tares, and bind them in bundles to burn them: but gather the wheat into my barn.*

The *reapers* are said in the explanation to be *the angels*; and they are represented as ministers of the great Judge of the world in the execution of his justice: And it appears, that both an executive power and discriminative knowledge is attributed to *them*. Civil magistrates in this world are denominated the ministers of God unto men for the

execution

execution of juftice. But the capacity of the wifeft and greateft among them is far inferior to that of the angels; and their power and office are, comparatively, of a very narrow extent. Superior beings have larger provinces affigned them, and a more ample cognizance and jurifdiction in refpect to mankind; yet fubject to the direction and appointment of the Savior and Sovereign of the world.

In the prefent ftate, notwithftanding all the meafures of divine Providence, and the endeavors of wife and good men, in order to promote juftice, reform the world, and eftablifh virtue, peace, and happinefs in it, many and great diforders will ever continue in human life. Mankind will always be, in fome meafure, corrupted, power abufed, innocence oppreffed, vice protected, the virtues of good men unrewarded, the crimes of the wicked unpunifhed, and grievances, offences, and temptations will abound. But all the evils of the world are only temporal; are permitted no longer than they anfwer the ends of divine wifdom and goodnefs, and fhall in due time be abolifhed: wickednefs and mifery fhall ceafe, and virtue and happinefs be for ever eftablifhed. The feries of events in human life is continually drawing nearer to a revolution. The period of time will at length arrive to every individual, when the Savior of the world will difcover and exert *his judicial and executive power* over his church and the whole world, that dominion over the confciences of mankind, that judgment of perfectly diftinguifhing the good from the evil, and that execution of eternally faving the one, and deftroying the other, which he hath in this parable afferted to himfelf; and which no other perfon or power can claim, without the higheft arrogance and impiety. But to him the Father Almighty hath committed it: *For the Father judgeth no man, but hath committed all judgment to the Son; that all men might honor the Son, even as they honor the Father;* **and that**

Separation of the Tares from the Wheat. 71
that in the end every knee might bow to him, and every tongue confefs, that JESUS CHRIST *is Lord, to the glory of God the Father.*

THIS divine defignation of our Savior to the high dignity and office of judging the world, CHRIST himfelf frequently reprefents to us in memorable figures:—As in Matthew xxv. 31. *When the Son of Man fhall come in his glory, and all his holy angels with him, then fhall he fit upon the throne of his glory; and before him fhall be gathered all nations; and he fhall feparate them one from another, as the fhepherd divideth his herds and flocks; and fhall fet the one on his right hand, and the other on his left. Then fhall the King fay unto them on his right hand, Come, ye bleffed of my Father,*—(where we may obferve, that fpeaking of himfelf in the third perfon, he gives to himfelf the title of King.)—In this parable he reprefents his own future power and judgment in a more familiar image: and having firft given to

F 4   himfelf

himself the character of the *sower*, who sowed good seed in the field of the world; then to preserve the propriety and consistency of the parable, he describes himself in the execution of the final judgment under the character of the *Lord of the harvest*, who commands the reapers to separate the tares, and bind them in bundles to be burned, and to gather the wheat into his garner.——In the explication, the familiarity of the images is converted into a more auguft and folemn manner of defcription. *The harveſt is the concluſion of the age, and the reapers are the angels. As therefore the tares are collected and conſumed in the fire; ſo ſhall it be at the concluſion of this life. The Son of man will ſend forth his angels; and they ſhall collect together out of his kingdom all things that offend, and them that do iniquity, and ſhall caſt them into the furnace of fire; there ſhall be weeping and gnaſhing of teeth. Then ſhall the righteous ſhine forth as the ſun in the kingdom of their Father.*

We

We are here led to the principal point of the whole parable, which will be the subject of another discourse.—In the mean time let us receive and digest the sentiments already explained. We live in a mixed state, where good and bad men grow promiscuously together. But it is not our province to judge the hearts of mankind around us. Let us study to approve ourselves to our own consciences, as sincere disciples of CHRIST. Let our profession and practice be consistent. Let the faith of the gospel be the master-spring of our actions. Let sincerity be our confidence, charity our honor, innocence and probity our ornament and defence. Let them be cultivated in us by a constant attention to the instructions and precepts of our holy religion. Then shall we be of the number of those *genuine Christians* whom our Savior came to *plant* in the world: And shall at last be distinguished by him and his angels,

angels, preserved from the destruction of the wicked, and advanced to the possession of his kingdom and glory. Which GOD of his infinite mercy grant, through *Jesus Christ* our LORD.

DISCOURSE IV.

Of the Harveſt: Or, Separation of the Tares from the Wheat.

Matthew xiii. 36. to 48.

Then Jesus sent the multitude away, and went into the house. And his disciples came unto him, saying, Declare unto us the parable of the tares of the field. He answered and said unto them: He that soweth the good seed is the Son of man: the field is the world: the good seed are the children of the kingdom: but the tares are the children of the wicked one: the enemy that sowed them is the devil: the harvest is the end of the world: and the reapers are the angels. As therefore the tares are gathered and burnt in the fire; so shall it be in the end of the world. The Son of man shall send forth his angels; and they shall gather out of his kingdom all things that offend, and them which do iniquity, and shall cast them into a furnace of fire: there shall be wailing and gnashing of teeth. Then shall the righteous shine forth as the sun in the kingdom of their Father.

IN the preceding discourse we first took a general view of the parable explained in the text, and then considered the several parts of it. It now remains, 3*dly*, that we attend to the principal point of the whole; which is the execution of the final judgment; or the separation of good and bad men; the destruction of the latter, and the preservation and happy establishment of the former, by the direction and authority of our Savior, as Judge of mankind in the future state.

A view of the corruptions of human nature and the evils of the world, hath tempted some to doubt of the moral character and government of the Maker of all things. Others have been led to arbitrary doctrines and groundless suppositions in order to reconcile thefe appearances with the divine perfections. Whilft others have wifely learned from them to know their own ignorance; and to confider how abfurd it is to expect that the plan of univerfal nature fhould be fuch as may be comprehended by the moft ignorant fpecies of rational creatures. Hence they have happily learned alfo to acquiefce in whatfoever the divine providence hath conftituted or permitted: and by attending to the many ftriking evidences of divine wifdom, juftice, and goodnefs, to encourage themfelves with a perfuafion, that all things tend to the greateft good. This is the wifeft improvement we can make of fuch a view: And all our experience and obfervation of the diforders and evils of this world have then their beft effect upon our minds, when they ferve to lead us to, or confirm us in, the faith and hope of the gofpel: namely, that all events tend to a glorious iffue; that there is a life to come, and a righteous judgment, when all diforders fhall be rectified,

tified, and all evils abolished. This is the sublime doctrine of our blessed Savior: To this happy consummation of events he directs our constant and most serious attention. All things in the creation answer the purposes of infinite wisdom: the wickedness of mankind is subservient to the righteousness of God; and the evils of the world conspire to the ends of his goodness: In what time and manner we cannot indeed comprehend. But it is our wisdom to look forward to futurity, and to wait with patience for the revelation of the righteous judgment of God.

In the mean time let us attend to the just and noble representations, which our Savior hath given us, of the state of mankind; the oeconomy of providence, the purpose of human life, and the conclusion of temporal events. From his discourses we may draw the clearest information in our religious enquiries, and the strongest encouragement to all virtue. Particularly,

Separation of the Tares from the Wheat.

in the parable explained in the text, he hath exhibited such a view of the state of the world, the design of providence, and the great revolution in which all the transactions of this life shall terminate, as may afford ample satisfaction to good men. For he instructs us, that GOD hath formed human nature, like the soil of the earth, capable of producing, by due culture, excellent and valuable fruits; but otherwise, yielding an unprofitable or noxious produce.—That it was his own peculiar care and labor, to cultivate the field of the world, and to make it productive of good men;—but that notwithstanding his endeavors it would still produce many bad men;—and that much art, industry, and malice would be employed, to corrupt mankind, and to propagate hypocrisy and wickedness.—And it is certain, that both good and bad men have arisen in every age and climate, in a greater or less abundance, in proportion to the endeavors of those, who have had it in their power, by their station and influence, to improve, or corrupt human nature, to promote knowledge or ignorance, to encourage virtue or vice.—The most distinguished and worthy characters that ever appeared in the world, have been those men, who, by their authority and example, their political and religious institutions, their maxims of wisdom and precepts of morality, have drawn the greatest numbers of mankind to piety and virtue. Many philosophers and lawgivers in former ages, more especially Moses and the other prophets of Jewish antiquity, are justly celebrated on this account; as being men eminently useful, not only in their own time, and to the people they were conversant with, but to remote nations and late posterity. They were then like skilful and diligent husbandmen, who endeavored, each according to his ability, to cultivate the field of the world, and to raise up and increase virtuous and good men in it. The same character belongs in a peculiar manner to our blessed Savior; who was not only

greater

greater in his perfonal capacity and authority, and more perfect in his example, but whose religious inftitutions and moral precepts flow from a fuperior wifdom, and have a more direct tendency to the improvement of mankind. He therefore juftly characterizes himfelf, by way of eminence and diftinction, *the fower* who fowed good feed in the field of the world; who employed his care and labor to produce good men in it. And his gofpel has in fact been the means of raifing up many excellent perfons: And would have had a much greater effect, and produced the beft kind of men in great abundance, if the world would have born them.—It may be probably fuppofed, befide other reafons, that providence permits the evils of the world, and the corruption and wickednefs of fome men, in order to exercife and improve the virtue and piety of others. And that the wifdom of GOD hath formed human nature like the foil of the earth, capable of yielding either a good or evil produce, on purpofe, purpose, that here might be a field for the exercise of those generous spirits, whose abilities shall qualify them, and whose benevolence shall excite them, to bestow labor and culture upon it.—However, our Savior appears to claim a property in, and dominion over the world of mankind: they are his field, territory, or kingdom, in which he exerted a most peculiar and distinguished virtue, in order to its improvement in the present state; and out of which he will finally extirpate, in a future state, all things useless and pernicious, destroy the workers of iniquity, preserve and promote good men, and establish perfect order and happiness. Then all present objections and perplexities will vanish; and the wisdom, justice, and goodness of the Almighty Maker of the world will appear with a superior evidence and unshaded lustre.

At present, and during the transitory scene of this life, mankind are subject to delusions, temptations, oppressions, and various

various other evils. Wickedness and misery pervade the human species, maintain a perpetual contest, and sometimes seem to prevail and rise superior to the peace and virtue of mankind. But is it the intention of the allwise Governor of the universe, to perpetuate the evils of the world, and to make wickedness and misery eternal? Nothing can be more repugnant to his justice and goodness, and to the supreme end of a divine government. For whatever wise reasons the evils of this world both natural and moral are permitted for a time and during the present scene, they shall not exist for ever: wickedness shall come to an end, and misery shall terminate in destruction: there shall be no more oppression or pain or death, evil shall cease, and perfect unmixed good prevail.—O glorious revolution! divine effect! worthy of an allwise being, agreeable to the highest conceptions we are able to form of perfect justice and goodness! worthy of the character, office, dignity, and empire of the

Son of God!—For this purpose he came into the world; to this end God raised him from the dead, exalted him to power and dominion, and committed to him all judgment over mankind: that he might at length purge the world from every corruption, abolish all evils, destroy the authors of them, and establish righteousness and happiness for ever. The angels shall collect together out of his kingdom *all things that offend*; *i. e.* whatever is a grievance, a snare, an occasion of wickedness and misery in the world. Good men shall then be no longer subject to those impositions by which they are at present liable to be hurt or seduced. Their faith and virtue shall stand secure from the assaults of temptation; every object or occasion of sin shall be abolished; and their integrity shall be no more exposed to those trials and dangers which occur in the present state. And further, the authors of evil, *the workers of iniquity*, shall likewise be destroyed for ever: they shall no longer exist to practise tife and propagate wickedness; to infest society, to violate the peace, and disturb the happiness of that everlasting kingdom. For, in like manner, as men separate and preserve the useful and valuable productions of nature, but throw useless and noxious materials into the fire to be consumed; *so shall it be at the conclusion of this life.* The good and valuable part of mankind shall be preserved, and possess the creation of GOD, and the kingdom of our Savior: But the worthless and wicked part be consumed with a horrible destruction, and never more exist. Then the world shall be delivered from every evil, and good become universal and eternal.

IT may assist us in forming some conceptions of the agency and authority of our Savior, in judging mankind, abolishing disorders and evils, destroying wicked men, and establishing the virtuous in a kingdom of order, peace and happiness; if we suppose a nation in this world sunk into corruption and flavery, laboring under various calamities and diforders, fubject to all the delufions and oppreffions of craft and tyranny; and then contemplate the kind providence of God raifing up for them an eminent deliverer, endued with a fingular wifdom, virtue and authority, in order to redeem them from their low and miferable eftate, to tranfplant them to a happier climate, to redrefs every grievance amongft them, to bring to juftice their corrupters and oppreffors, to feparate and exterminate them that are unworthy to live, and to eftablifh the reft in perfect order, fecurity and tranquillity. Thus (if we may compare fmall things to great, and a temporal to an eternal deliverance) the wifdom of the Father Almighty hath proceeded in refpect to the whole world and final ftate of mankind; hath raifed up from the dead his Anointed, and exalted him, becaufe he was worthy, to be the fovereign and Savior of the world, to give life to the dead, to reward all men according to their deferts, deserts, to exerminate the wicked, to deliver the good from all temptations and evils, and to establish them in a kingdom that shall never be moved, that kingdom which was designed and prepared for them from the foundation of the world.

THIS renovation or new establishment of the world of mankind is prefigured in various prophetical passages of the holy scriptures: *First*, tho' more obscurely, by the prophets in the Old Testament, who foretel and describe the character, office, kingdom, and glory of the *Messiah*: more plainly by *John the Baptist*: still more so so by our *Savior* himself: and lastly by his apostles. For our Savior, his forerunner, and his apostles, plainly make the requisite and important distinction, which the prophets of old did not clearly express, between the first coming and final appearance of CHRIST; and describe the latter as the great design and effect of his enterprize. With this view, his harbinger John the

Baptist

Baptist thus characterizes him: *There cometh one after me who is mightier than I, whose shoes I am not worthy to unloose; whose fan is in his hand, and he will throughly purge his floor, and will gather up his wheat into the garner, and burn up the chaff with unquenchable fire.*——Our Savior in this parable and many other discourses, represents the same grand revolution and happy renovation of all things at *the end of the world*, or, *the conclusion of this life*, as the main design and effect of his coming; to which all that he did and suffered on earth, even his dying and rising from the dead, was no more than an introduction or preparation; that so he might become the author of our eternal salvation. It is in this character of final judge and sovereign of the world, that he most frequently describes himself. The future state of mankind is his *kingdom*; that kingdom of heaven which he so often represents by various familiar figures and resemblances. The importance and effect of his enterprize consist, not so much in what he he hath already done, as in what he will hereafter accomplish. His appearance in this world, his wise instructions, his exemplary virtue, his mighty miracles, his visible resurrection from the dead and ascension to heaven, were but as it were a preliminary condition, a short preface, an imperfect sketch or specimen, in order to that dominion which he hath acquired, that office which he executes, and that scene of glory which he will disclose at his second appearance; when he shall come to be admired of his followers, and to execute justice on them who know not God, and that obey not his gospel. When he was on earth, he healed the sick, restored the maimed, gave sight to the blind, and sense to the distracted, and raised the dead to life: He instructed the ignorant, reproved the wicked, and preached the gospel to the poor: He reformed the world, as far as the most excellent instructions and example, enforced by a series of beneficent miracles, would operate in a way of persuasion

suasion and encouragement. In the other world then, when by his potent voice men shall awake from the dead and rise to another life; what wonders will he perform? with what wisdom and authority will he speak? what goodness and beneficence will he discover? How perfect a reformation of mankind will he accomplish; when in virtue of his high dominion and office, he shall separate the just from the unjust, destroy the workers of iniquity, abolish all evils, and throughly establish his kingdom; an entire world of virtue and happiness? when *he shall send forth his angels; and they shall collect together out of his kingdom all things that offend, and them that do iniquity; and shall throw them into the furnace of fire,* in order to their total abolition: and when *the righteous shall shine forth as the sun in the kingdom of their Father.*

To this blest change, this new-born state of life and happiness, all faithful Christians aspire with warm affection and earnest expectation,

pectation, as the subject of their best hopes, and the summit of their highest wishes.—It may be said of mankind in general, that being conscious of, and laboring under the disorders and evils of the present state, they are waiting with some degree of apprehension, and hope, of a better state after death. *For the earnest expectation of the creature,* (says the apostle) *i. e.* of the species of mankind, *waiteth for the manifestation of the sons of God*; *i. e.* the discovery of the future state of good men. *For the creature, i. e.* the species, *was made subject to vanity, i. e.* to corruption and dissolution: *not willingly, i. e.* not by their own choice; *but by him who subjected it, i. e.* by the appointment of divine providence. *It waiteth in hope, that the creature itself, i. e.* even the species in general, *shall be set free from the slavery of corruption into the glorious liberty of the children of God. For we know that the whole creation* (or, as it is in the margin, every creature, *i. e.* mankind in general) *groaneth and travaileth in pain together*

together even to this time: not only so, but even ourselves, who have the first fruits of the spirit, even we apostles *groan within ourselves, waiting for the adoption, the redemption of our body*; *i. e.* our deliverance from this bodily state, and becoming invested with a body incorruptible and immortal. But having the expectation and hope of so glorious a change; *the light afflictions of the present time, which are but,* as it were, *for a moment, are not worthy to be compared to the far more exceeding and eternal weight of glory which shall be* hereafter disclosed. Under every present oppression then, or gloomy appearance of things around us, what can so much relieve the mind and inspire great and pleasing hopes, as that prospect of the future judgment, and the new establishment of the world of mankind, which our Savior has presented to us in natural and lively figures? When the evils of the world, which are permitted for wise ends, and for the present time only, shall serve to make the divine justice and goodness the more conspicuous,

conspicuous, in the sight of the whole intelligent creation. The time of this life is but a short period: a thousand years is but as a moment compared to the ages of eternity. If then there are many difficulties and trials to be met with in this local and temporary constitution of nature; if good men sometimes taste the bitter cup of adversity, or are surrounded with snares and enemies; here is the proof of their integrity: this is the field of warfare, in which they are to exercise their prudence, fortitude, patience, benevolence to men, and confidence in GOD: that so *the trial of their faith*, their fidelity and virtue, *being more precious than that of gold, may be found unto praise, honor and glory, at the revelation of Jesus Christ.*—How many and great soever *the afflictions of the righteous* man are, *the Lord will deliver him out of them all*, and establish him in *a place* of safety and honor, from whence he shall *behold the destruction of the wicked, but it shall not come nigh* him. When the proud oppressors of the

the earth and crafty seducers of mankind, who have sought only to gratify their insatiable lusts of pleasure, wealth and power, shall become objects of horror and contempt, and be *thrown into the furnace of destruction*: when the *poor of this world being rich in faith* shall possess *the kingdom prepared* for them: when the oppressed shall be delivered, and the lowly exalted: when the worthy shall be promoted, and the followers of CHRIST in virtue, piety, and patience shall partake of *his* glory and joy. When the powers of this world which have supported and propagated superstition, impiety and wickedness, oppressed the innocent, condemned the just, persecuted the adherents of true religion, and cruelly adjudged them to perish in flames of fire, shall themselves be arraigned before a superior judge, condemned by a most just sentence, and doomed to perish in fire unquenchable;—then, all evils and the authors of them being totally abolished, *the new world* will be established; a world of good

good without evil, of life free from death, of activity without weariness, of enjoyment without suffering, of virtue unpolluted with vice, of love untainted with hatred, of honor unenvyed, and happiness uninterrupted. Then *the kingdom of God and of his Christ* will be fully come; *that kingdom* which he hath foretold and described, to which he directs our most earnest attention, and to establish which was the great end of all his labors, and the supreme object of his view and desire: *that kingdom* which he will *present to God, even the Father* Almighty, and in which he will *put down all rule and all authority and power*, and subdue every thing to *himself*. For in the highest exertion of his power and grandeur of his empire, when all things are become subject unto him, then *shall the Son himself be* nevertheless *subject* to the will of the Father Almighty, who gave him *this kingdom* and glory, *that God may be all in all.*

Now *seeing we look for such things; what manner of persons ought we to be* in the cultivation and practice of all virtue? that we may be found of him in peace at his appearance?—Let us by a *patient continuance in well-doing seek for glory, honor, and immortality.* If we know how to make use of the disorders and temptations of the present life, so as to exercise our faith, fortitude, temperance, probity, and charity; then it will be most happy for us, that ever we were born into this world;—*this world*, which some are so apt to complain of, others to over-value, and all to abuse. The end of human life is the great object of every wise man's attention: And there is nothing so momentous in itself, yet so little considered, as that life or death eternal is before us; and that our present conduct will affect our future condition, and draw after it everlasting consequences.

Now that we may *know the things that belong to our peace* and safety, *before they be be hid from our eyes;* and may so improve the short time that we are to remain in this world, as to be found worthy to obtain that life and world which are eternal, GOD grant of his infinite mercy through *Jesus Christ* our LORD.

DISCOURSE V.

Of the Net which gathered of every Kind: Or, the Capture and Aſſortment of Fiſhes.

Matthew xiii. 47.

Again the kingdom of heaven is like unto a net which was cast into the sea, and gathered of every kind; which, when it was full, they drew to the shore, and having sat down, they gathered the good into vessels, but cast the bad away.—So shall it be at the end of this world: the angels shall come forth and sever the wicked from among the just, and shall cast them into the furnace of fire: there shall be weeping and gnashing of teeth.

THE great prophet of God and Savior of the world is here instructing his immediate disciples, and raising their minds to some apprehension of a subject the most important and interesting to mankind;

mankind; to reveal and publish which to the world was a peculiar and principal part of his prophetic office. And if we consider how difficult it is to raise ignorant minds, accustomed only to low notions, and possessed by strong prejudices, to a knowledge of spiritual and sublime things; we shall perceive the wisdom of our Savior in unfolding to them *the mysteries of the kingdom of heaven* so gradually, and by figurative and parabolical representations, such as were proper to excite their attention and curiosity, and likewise to inform their understandings, as far as the weakness of their minds would permit. Yet these parables are of such a construction, that the more enlightened our understandings are, and the more free from prejudice; the more shall we admire the simplicity and beauty of them, and receive with the higher approbation the great truths intended to be conveyed by them.

Our Lord had before delivered to the people the parable of *the tares of the field,* of which his disciples, as soon as they were apart from the multitude, and in private with him, earnestly desired an explanation; which he condescended to give them; and added also some other parables, particularly this of the text, in order to accustom them to such kind of representations, to enliven their attention to them, and as a further explanation of the main subject intended in them. But after all, it does not appear, that he designed to express his sense in the clearest manner; but rather to furnish matter for their future study and reflexion. For when he asked them, if they understood these things; though they replyed, *Yea, Lord*; yet it is most probable, that their knowledge of his meaning was very imperfect and confused: and that their answer proceeded rather from a shame of confessing their ignorance, than any clear apprehension of the grandeur and extent of his ideas. It was not till after his resurrection from the dead, and the effusion of the Holy Spirit, that they attained

tained to a thorow comprehenſion of his doctrine; when all the important inſtructions he had before given them were brought to remembrance, and their underſtandings were prepared to receive them.

When they firſt became his followers, they expected that he would riſe to worldly greatneſs, become king of the Jews, and conqueror of the Roman empire: And nothing was further from their thoughts, at that time, than to imagine, that inſtead of this, he was to die, riſe from the dead to an immortal life, and become the Sovereign and Judge of mankind in another world. Of this they ſeem not to have had the leaſt conception: On the contrary, when he intimated theſe things to them, it ſeems to have overpowered their feeble minds, and to have confounded their apprehenſions of him. Or if they did attain to ſome faint ideas of his future eternal dominion; yet they did not doubt but that he would firſt become a mighty prince on earth: And this

this prejudice adhered to them till his death, and seems to have been revived, in some measure, after his resurrection, when they asked him, *Lord, wilt thou at this time restore the kingdom to Israel?*

There was another great prejudice also common to the Jews at that time, and which subsists at this day in the minds of many persons; which was, a strong presumption, that the Messiah, or Christ, when he came, would not only erect a government on earth, but in consequence of it, reform mankind, redress grievances, administer justice, make all his followers virtuous and happy, and in a word, establish peace and good order throughout the world.—This prejudice was naturally connected with the former. For as on the one hand, the greatest order and peace of human society might be expected from a perfect government; so on the other, no means appear to be so effectual to reform nations, and establish the happiness of human

man life, as such a government; in which justice shall be so thorowly administred, that every person, of whatsoever rank and condition, shall be visibly rewarded, or punished, according to his behavior. But as this scheme does not appear to have been the plan and purpose of divine providence, in the formation of this world and of human nature, so neither was it the design and end of our Savior's coming. The wisdom of GOD thought fit to commit the government of nations, the direction of all civil affairs, and the administration of justice in society, to men themselves: And it was not our LORD's design to change this plan, to deprive princes and governors of their dominion, to assume civil power, and set up a supernatural government on earth. For though the popes of Rome have expresly assumed such a temporal dominion above all other princes, by a pretended authority from CHRIST; yet he himself expresly disclaimed it. For in contradiction to the above-mentioned prejudices,

dices, he declares in one place, that *his kingdom was not of this world:* i. e. the power and empire to which he pretended were wholly in another world. And in another place, that *he was not come to send peace on earth,* or to eſtabliſh the order and happineſs of human ſociety: beſide many other paſſages, in which he foretells and deſcribes the corruptions, diſorders, and perſecutions which would ariſe in the world, and which, inſtead of being prevented, or remedied, would rather, in ſome inſtances, be occaſioned, or aggravated, by the publication of the goſpel. Particularly, in the foregoing parable of the tares, he not only prefigures himſelf in the great character of proprietor of the *field*, which is the *world*, and ſovereign diſpoſer of its various produce; but foretells, that though he had ſown in it *good ſeed,* yet the ſpirit of enmity to the goſpel, a ſpirit of hypocriſy and wickedneſs, would ſteal in, as it were in the night, and would ſow tares, which would grow up among the wheat, and would be so intermixed, that the proper time of separation could not be till the *harvest*: the meaning of which is, that good and bad men would always arise together in the world, and be so intermingled, even in the Christian world, that a separate judgment could not be properly made in this life: But at the time of *harvest*, at the conclusion of life, when the proper *season* was come, he would *say to the reapers, Gather up the tares and bind them in bundles to burn them, but gather the wheat into my garner:* which is thus expressed in the explanation. *The Son of man will send forth his angels, and they shall gather out of his kingdom all things that offend and them that do iniquity, and shall cast them into a furnace of fire: there shall be weeping and gnashing of teeth.*

It was proper to repeat so much of the parable of the tares; as this in the text was evidently designed to convey to his disciples the same meaning with that. Only

Only it may be obferved, that *here* he entirely omits his own character and agency in that tranfaction, which he intended to prefigure, and prefents to view only the final diftinction and feparation of good and bad men. This omiffion was defigned, as feems probable, out of condefcenfion to the weaknefs of his difciples, who could hardly, at that time, conceive of him, in the fublime quality of Judge of mankind, in refpect to a future and eternal ftate. He therefore reduces the fubject to a greater fimplicity, and confines his allufion to the final feparation between good men and bad, by the cognizance and judgment of fuperior Beings denominated the angels: And he makes ufe of the figure of *a net caft into the fea*, as being very familiar to his difciples, who were fome of them *fifhermen*. As the lower animals are in refpect to mankind, fuch are men themfelves compared to the angels: And thofe fuperior Beings underftand the difference of good men and bad, and are capable of diftinguifhing and

feparating

separating them, as the *shepherd* is of dividing his *flocks and herds,* or the *fisherman* of distinguishing the different species of *fishes* taken together in his net. They know which sort of men are fit to be preserved, and which to be destroyed, and, at the conclusion of the age, shall come forth and sever the wicked from among the just, and shall cast them into a furnace of fire, to be utterly consumed.

The kingdom of heaven, therefore, or the future state, *is like unto a net which was cast into the sea, and gathered of every kind:* For all men shall be raised from the dead, every one in his own order, and all pass into the future state. But as the net, when it was full, was drawn to the shore, and they sat down to examine their capture, and *separated the good into vessels, and cast the bad away; so shall it be at the conclusion of the age.* Good men and bad are equally subject to death, and shall *both* pass from the state of the dead to another life: But

notwith-

notwithstanding, *both* shall not be saved: a scrutiny shall commence, their different qualities shall be distinguished, an impartial judgment passed, and a final separation made. They who are found *worthy*, as our Lord expresseth it, *of that world and the resurrection from the dead*, shall be preserved in eternal life; but they who are judged to be unworthy of life, or not fit to be saved, shall be destroyed. As men distinguish, select, and carefully preserve things of value, or which are fit for some good use and purpose, but cast away things that are vile and useless, or consume them in the fire; mankind themselves shall be disposed of in the future state according to the same method and rule, by the distinguishing judgment of superior beings, under the direction of our Savior, who is the Lord and Judge of all. Men's respective qualifications and deserts shall be most impartially considered; and they who are found to be unqualified for eternal life and unworthy of salvation, shall be cast away as vile and useless, and exposed to perish for ever; shall not be suffered to live or exist any longer; but be thrown, as it were, into a furnace of fire, in order to their total destruction. And lest we should vainly imagine, that the punishment of wicked men shall be a mere deprivation of life and being, without proportionate degrees of pain and misery, our Savior expressly adds, *there shall be wailing and gnashing of teeth:* an expression which implies dreadful and excruciating agonies. These miseries shall undoubtedly be in exact proportion to the crimes men have committed and the measure of guilt they have contracted. *The servant who knew his Lord's will but did it not,* who transgressed knowingly, purposely, maliciously, shall suffer *more stripes,* than he who sinned rather thro' ignorance and folly than presumption and obstinacy. Yet there appears no reason to doubt, but that the punishment of every condemned criminal shall be great, and the period of his eternal destruction dreadful

dreadful beyond expression. For *when* once *the master of the house is risen up, and hath shut the door, and they begin to stand without and say, Lord, Lord, open unto us, and he shall say to them, I know you not; depart from me, ye workers of iniquity; then shall be wailing and gnashing of teeth*—then *when they shall see Abraham, Isaac, and Jacob, and all the prophets in the kingdom of God, and themselves shut out: when they shall see many come from the east and the west, the north and the south,* from all parts of the world, and admitted into the community and habitation of the blessed, while *themselves are excluded: when* they shall see many whom they despised in this world, as beneath their notice, *shining forth as the sun,* in the mansions of light and glory, from which themselves are for ever debarred: *when* all protection, all safety and hope shall be withdrawn from them: *when* with ardent eyes they shall see the inestimable prize of eternal life, and with the utmost vehemence of passion desire to obtain it, but in vain:

when

when the agonies of defpair and of death eternal fhall feize them, and they fhall feel the infupportable weight of almighty power precipitating them into the abyfs of everlafting deftruction. Such punifhment, fo dreadful a period may well be thought fufficient to fatisfy divine juftice and to anfwer the ends of divine government. And the denunciation of a judgment fo awful, a mifery fo infupportable, a ruin fo irrecoverable, fhould in reafon be more than fufficient to deter all men, who have the leaft degree of fober reflexion and confideration, from the practice of wickednefs; to awaken the moft fecure and thoughtlefs, and to reclaim the moft obftinate and hardened. Need we then to fuppofe, that God will preferve condemned finners in life and being for ever, in order to make their wickednefs and mifery endlefs? Can it be confiftent with reafon, juftice, or goodnefs, needlefsly to prolong and increafe wickednefs and mifery? Can this be the purpofe or defire of any good Being?

Is

Is it not the ftrongeft and moft natural defire of every good mind to diminifh the quantity of evil in the world, and to put a ftop, as far as is poffible, to wickednefs and mifery? What can be more grateful, then, to the heart of a good man, than to be affured by the gofpel, that a final period fhall be put to the wickednefs and mifery of the world? and that virtue and happinefs *alone* fhall remain *for ever*, and be propagated and increafed to everlafting ages?—Glorious and happy revolution! which fhall take place at the fecond coming of our Lord and Savior; when he fhall come with his mighty angels, and eftablifh the throne of his government over the world of mankind; when he fhall adminfter impartial juftice; when he fhall fever the wicked from amongft the righteous, and punifh them with *an everlafting deftruction from his prefence and by his glorious power*; when he fhall abolifh all evils, and make an utter end of wickednefs and mifery; when *death and hell fhall be caft into the lake of fire*, and there shall be no more sin, nor sorrow, nor pain, nor death; when *all things* shall be made *new*, an intire world established, wherein no evil shall take root, but virtue, peace, and happiness grow and flourish for ever. This is *the everlasting kingdom of our Lord and Savior, out of which all things that offend and they that do iniquity* shall be extirpated, and into which nothing shall enter *that defileth, or that maketh a lye,* nothing that is deformed or deceitful. As then the fisherman draws his net when it is full to the shore, and separates the good into vessels, but casts the bad away; as the husbandman separates the wheat from the tares, and carefully preserves the former, but burns up the latter; as the master of a feast admits the worthy guests, but excludes the unworthy; as the prince rewards his faithful servants, but commands the rebellious to be brought forth and slain in his presence;—so shall it be at the conclusion of human life.——

THESE natural images and allusions were intended by our Savior to impress upon our minds the most lively idea of the final distinction and separation which shall be made between good and bad men; when the former shall be put in possession of a world of everlasting life; but the latter be excluded, cast away, put to death eternal, utterly consumed, as it were, in an unquenchable fire. There will then be no place for repentance, nor will any intreaties or supplications have any effect. For when once *the master of the house is risen up and hath shut the door,* there can be no admittance, and in vain shall they stand without, saying, *Lord, Lord, open unto us;* and tho' they should plead " *we have eaten* " *and drank in thy presence, and thou hast* " *taught in our streets,*" the answer will be, " *I know not whence ye are, depart* " *from me ye that work iniquity.*" No petitions or pleas will avail to alter the sentence of the great Judge of the world; no possibility remain of escaping the impending

pending ruin. And when they shall see that kingdom of heaven, that world of immortality, from which they are for ever shut out; and know the infinite value of that eternal life, which they have lost, by their own folly and wickedness; this sight, and this knowledge, will necessarily aggravate their misery, and fill them with inconsolable regret and horror. To be condemned by a human judicature, and put to death in this world, as criminals unfit for society and unworthy of life; to be made examples of punishment, and exposed as spectacles of disgrace and ruin, is a scene full of horror and misery. But no sufferings in this world, no temporal death, can be supposed equal to the misery and destruction of sinners in another world, condemned to death eternal.

If then we have any concern to avoid the greatest misery and most terrible destruction that can befal us; if our own eternal life and safety be dear to us; if we have

have any defire of immortality, and put any value upon the glory and happinefs of an everlafting world;—let us avoid guilt, and be afraid to commit iniquity: let us flee from it, *as from the face of a ferpent, whofe fting is fharper than a two-edged fword, and whofe teeth are as the teeth of a lion flaying the fouls of men.* Let the fteddy belief of an everlafting ftate, of the final feparation of good and evil men, of the eternal falvation of the former and deftruction of the latter, be an invincible guard to repel temptations and to defend and maintain our integrity; and an effectual motive to the practice of all virtue: That fo *the trial of our faith being more precious than gold, may be found unto praife, honor, and glory, at the coming of our Savior Jefus Chrift.*

DISCOURSE VI.

Of the Treasure hid in a Field: And the Pearl of great Price.

Matthew xiii. 44.

Again, the kingdom of heaven is like unto treasure hid in a field; which when a man hath found he hideth, and for joy thereof goeth and selleth all that he hath, and buyeth that field. Again, the kingdom of heaven is like unto a merchant-man seeking goodly pearls: who when he had found one pearl of great price, he went and sold all that he had and bought it.

THESE two parables are proper to be taken into consideration jointly; as they have both apparently the same meaning, and were intended to represent, under similar figures, the excellence and value of the kingdom of heaven, or the future state of happiness. In one instance, the

the worth of it is compared to *treasure hid in a field*; in the other to *a pearl of great price*. Thus our Savior by familiar images adapted to the capacity, temper, and affections of his disciples, raises their minds to an high esteem of that glorious eternal kingdom, which he was to establish in another world. In other discourses and allusions he instructs them as to the *nature* of it, and describes the *qualifications* for possessing it: In these, he illustrates, in a comparative view, its supreme *value*. As the gross conceptions of mankind are not easily raised to things abstract, sublime and spiritual, nor indeed is human language sufficient to convey proper notions of those things which *eye hath not seen, nor ear heard, nor have entred into the heart of man*; therefore he makes use of those sensible objects, which the eye of man hath seen, and the ear heard of, and the imagination been affected with; in order to excite our desire and pursuit of heavenly and invisible things. Hence, the happiness of another life is figured

red to us in the New Teftament by treafures, entertainments, fplendors, crowns, inheritances, and the like. Such reprefentations fhould not be confidered, as debafing the dignity of thefe fubjects, but as the wifeft and fitteft means of rendering them intelligible, and reducing them to a level with the low underftandings and earthly apprehenfions of men. For a revelation from heaven addreffed to mankind muft make ufe of the common language and ideas of men, in order to become intelligible, and operate upon their defires and affections. It is an argument therefore of the wifdom of our Savior and propriety of his difcourfes, that in treating of fpiritual and invifible things, he has conftant recourfe to material and vifible objects, and applies them in a manner fo proper to imprefs the fentiment which he intended, with as much force and clearnefs, as the capacities of his difciples would admit. Intending therefore to reprefent the ineftimable value of the kingdom of heaven, in

a

a manner proper to quicken their attention and raife their defires, he compares it to *treafure hid in a field*; *which, when a man hath found,* he becomes elevated with the joyful difcovery, and employs all his thought and concern how to become poffeffed of it. In the other figure, which ftands in connexion with this, he pourtraits his difciples in the habit and appearance of *merchants,* travelling thro' different countries, and fearching for *pearls*; and when they have found one of the higheft value, making ufe of all their abilities, and parting with every thing elfe, in order to purchafe it. Thus, with the fimplicity of a divine art, he awakens the curiofity of his difciples, by defcribing the kingdom of heaven as an *hidden treafure,* and a *pearl* that muft be *fought* for in order to be found. He takes hold alfo of that defire of acquiring property, and of gaining fplendid poffeffions, which is fo natural, and which had no fmall influence on their minds. For it appears very evident from the hiftory, story, that the apoſtles themſelves followed our Savior, at firſt, chiefly from a motive of curioſity, or from lucrative expectations. He ſpeaks therefore with a condeſcending regard to their errors and prejudices, as well as to the weakneſs and groſſneſs of all human apprehenſion. *They*, like the reſt of *mankind*, wanted to become rich, great, and happy in the world: and like the reſt of the *Jews*, never doubted but their Meſ-ſiah would become a temporal prince; and if they could be firſt in his favor, expected all ſorts of worldly preferments, from his power and liberality. Hence ſprung emulations and contentions amongſt them, which of them ſhould have the preference in his eſteem, ſit at his right hand, and be the greateſt in his kingdom. Hence alſo the melancholy and deſpair which ſeized them, when his death deſtroyed their worldly hopes.—It is worth our cloſeſt attention to obſerve the candor, prudence, reſerve, propriety and addreſs by which our Lord gradually weaned them from their

Vol. III.   K   prejudices,

prejudices, and directed their hopes and desires to that future state, which he denoted by the kingdom of heaven.—For though they had but faint apprehensions of a life to come, and followed him at first, with no other than worldly views and hopes; yet *at length*, he fully convinced them, that he *had indeed a kingdom*, though *not of this world*, a kingdom of truth and virtue on earth, and of eternal life and glory in another world. Then they found the *hidden treasure*, they discovered the *pearl of great price*; and became so animated with the rich discovery, that they went and sold all that they had to secure the possession: *for joy thereof* they abandoned every thing in the world, in order to become heirs of eternal life. After the resurrection of Christ and his ascent to heaven, their sentiments, views and hopes became entirely changed; they were no longer men of this world, but of another; they looked not at things temporal, but things eternal; their discourses and actions discover

cover a spirit above all regard to the riches and pleasures of this world, and wholly intent upon those treasures in heaven, that eternal kingdom and joy of their Lord, which he had propounded to them, and on which he had gradually led them to fix their strongest affections and hopes.

So in regard to the condition and character of mankind in general, and of Christians in particular, in all ages—They are full of worldly notions and passions, are chiefly intent upon erecting for themselves a scheme of temporal prosperity and happiness, think but little of another world, and have scarce the least affection, desire, or hope tending that way;—till by some powerful means or happy event, their apprehensions are awakened, their dreams about worldly pleasures and preferments vanish, and the faith of the gospel enters into their hearts, and begins to operate upon their affections and actions. Then their errors are rectified, they understand things in another manner, they see life in a different light,—an eternal world stands disclosed, and in full view before them,—they behold it, and are astonished at the reality, the nearness, and the grandeur of the object; and its infinite importance and value excite their strongest desires and hopes. Here is a *treasure*, which before lay concealed from their notice. They had been in search after real happiness and a substantial good, equal to their largest desires; but had sought for it, where it was not to be found: *here* it is at length discovered, where they had never searched for it, nor believed that any thing existed worthy of their regard: but they are now convinced, that here lies the only real inexhaustible fund of wealth, honor, and happiness. The discovery fills them with admiration and joy: and now they seek in the first place *the kingdom of GOD and the righteousness thereof*; and are content to forego all other things in order to secure this inestimable possession: they reflect with regret

regret upon their former blindnefs and inattention, their dark and wandering purfuits after thofe delufive treafures, which vanifh like fmoke, or at beft, perifh in the ufing; while they were negligent and unapprized of the only folid and lafting good.

Let us confider a while the nature of thofe objects which men ordinarily purfue, on the miftaken fchemes of ignorance, vanity, or vice. Some are captivated with fenfitive pleafures, and the gratifications of bodily eafe and appetite: Others with appearances of pomp, and the furniture and trappings of worldly diftinction. Some are feized with a fpirit of domination; and the higheft good they aim at is to bear rule, to controul, to fubdue, to erect a petty kingdom for the exercife of their own refentful and imperious paffions: Others are fubject to the fordid luft of avarice; and the object of all their defires is a ufelefs growing load of earthly property. Thefe feveral several desires and pursuits, though they seem widely different from each other, yet all terminate alike; as they are all bounded within the limits of this life; and as the goods, they respectively aim at, are equally deceitful, unsatisfying, and transitory. Men addicted to these different pursuits mutually despise and condemn each other: the epicure on the one hand, and the miser on the other; the man of ease and gaiety, and the man of industry and ambition, throw the censure of folly on each other, for mistaking and neglecting their own happiness: And it is with equal reason on all sides that they thus accuse each other. For assuredly, the error and folly, if not the guilt, is equal in them all; and none of them have yet discovered where the good of mankind lyes: they know neither the nature nor the place thereof: it is hid from their eyes: and their erroneous pursuits have only led them the further from it: all their searches have been in reality fruitless: they have either found nothing, or have

have been deluded with an imaginary *treasure*, a *counterfeit pearl of no price.* O capital mistake, fatal delusion! proceeding from a false judgment and a depraved mind. *The light of the body is the eye: and if thine eye be single, thy whole body shall be full of light: but if thine eye be evil, thy whole body shall be full of darkness.* If the discerning sense and judgment of the mind concerning the nature and value of things be itself blind, *how great is that darkness!*

But when the eye of the understanding is cleared from distemper, when the judgment is freed from vicious prejudices, and so rectified as to discern the true nature and comparative worth of different things; when the faith of the gospel, that sovereign medicine of human reason, has purged the mental sight, and enabled it to take a prospective view beyond the limits of human life; then all things stand confessed in their proper shape, color, and magnitude: the mind becomes capable of measuring things by a certain compafs, of weighing them in a juſt ballance, and trying them by the touchſtone of truth, in order to determine their intrinſic value. And the compariſon is no ſooner made between temporal poſſeſſions and the inheritance of an immortal life, between the ſhort-lived gains and gratifications of ſin, and the eternal rewards of virtue, between the kingdoms of this world and the everlaſting kingdom of our Lord and Savior; but the infinite difference becomes apparent, and ſtrikes the diſcerning mind with an irreſiſtible conviction. The falſe color and fictitious value of earthly things are detected;—they are known to be but droſs and tinſel, and the value of eternal things is underſtood to be real and ineſtimable.

But it is with great difficulty, and often by ſlow degrees that men are brought to give any real attention to another world, and place their views and hopes upon it. The things of this world are preſent to the

ſenſes

senses from the beginning of life; and the cares, passions, and views which they raise in the mind are of early date, and speedy growth; and often gain so entire a possession of the heart as to exclude all attention to, and prospect of, eternal things. It is a mighty effort of reason, and stretch of the discerning faculty, to extend a view beyond death to another life, and to act upon the belief of a world invisible. Such conduct implies a soundness of judgment, an extensive thought and design, a wise foresight, a steady resolution, and a superiority to sensual passions and earthly prejudices. But few attain to such an elevation and strength of mind: most men have their understandings and affections chiefly confined within the limits of this life, and hardly extend a thought beyond. They must first meet with worldly disappointments, find their vanity mortified, their expectations frustrated, and the lofty structure of temporal felicity, which they had built for themselves in their own imagination,

nation, demolished. They must first taste the gall that is intermixed with human delights, and experience the care and vexation of spirit which attend worldly pursuits. They must feel the loss of friends, relations, riches, honors, and other external acquisitions, and perhaps of health also, before they will vouchsafe to take another world into consideration: And then, when they can no longer enjoy this world, when they are convinced by woeful experience, that happiness is not to be attained in this life; they are compelled, as it were by necessity, to look forward, and apply their thoughts to a future state: then they grow serious and devout; and would gladly rectify, in the decline of life, the errors and follies of their former days: they begin to wish for the happiness of a life to come, and to seek for the kingdom of God and the righteousness thereof: but the season is late; and the noble improvements, which might have been made in earlier life, are lost. Vicious and worldly habits

habits leave also an unhappy tincture behind them, and fill the mind with regret: And tho' men are at last convinced, that there is an hidden treasure beyond the grave, and that the real happiness of mankind lies there; they find it exceedingly difficult to fix their hearts upon it, and like the apostles, for joy thereof to resign whatever may stand in competition with it. How much better would it be, if men would, *in the first place*, seek for this kingdom of heaven, without loss of time, without misapplication of talents, without the correction of worldly disappointments. How happy if from a sound judgment and diligent search they would find the *hidden treasure*; and animated with the joyful discovery, would make it the chief business of their whole lives to gain it—if with the spirit of men contending in a race, they would press forward with all their might towards the mark, for the prize of the high calling of God in Christ Jesus? If without vainly attempting to lay up for ourselves

selves a precarious treasure of good things in this world, we would immediately study to lay up for ourselves *a treasure in heaven, where no thief approacheth nor rust corrupteth*; which is subject to no invasion, no decay! How insecure is the property of worldly things! how unsatisfying the enjoyment of them! how little real happiness is to be extracted from them! how much vexation and anxiety do they sometimes create! what pain and regret is often produced by an excessive pursuit of them! how soon shall we be forced to abandon them, and be driven away, despoiled of all, into an unknown eternal state!

If ever we shall be so happy as to obtain the life to come, and to possess the real and durable treasures of the other world; how shall we then reflect upon the weak and childish prejudices which had so much influence upon us in this life? how shall we be amazed at the passionate folly with which we pursued the trifles of this world?

how

how shall we condemn our blindness and inattention to things of such superior excellence and of eternal duration? Earthly possessions, even all the kingdoms of this world and the glory of them, will then appear as mean and insignificant, as the toys and amusements of our infant ignorance and vanity.—Or if (which may God prevent) thro' greediness of appetite and covetous desires after the mean possessions and pleasures of this world, we lose the favor of our almighty Father, and forfeit our eternal inheritance; what regret, what inconsolable despair must ensue! But if we are so faithful in the *unrighteous mammon*, as to gain the *true riches*; so prudent in the use of the little things, which are *lent* us for a short time, as to obtain those things which shall be *our own* for ever; so careful as to discover the *hidden wealth*, and find the *one pearl of great price*; and so wise, as to renounce every interest or pleasure that stands in competition with it;—

then

then shall we be rich indeed;—the treasure will be inexhaustible, the property secure, and the joy thereof inexpressible and eternal: Which GOD of his infinite mercy grant through *Jesus Christ* our LORD.

DISCOURSE VII.

Of the Grain of Muſtard-ſeed, which became the greateſt of Herbs: and the Leaven which diffuſed itſelf through the whole Maſs.

DISCOURSE VII.

Of the Church Multiplied, when became the greatest in Heroes, and the Lamb, which defeated it all, was the whole Rule.

MATTHEW xiii. 31.

Another parable put he forth unto them, saying, The kingdom of heaven is like to a grain of mustard-seed, which a man took and sowed in his field; which indeed is the least of all seeds; but when it is grown it is the greatest amongst herbs, and becometh a tree; so that the birds of the air come and lodge in the branches thereof.——Another parable spake he unto them: The kingdom of heaven is like unto leaven, which a woman took and hid in three measures of meal till the whole was leavened.

THE parables of our Savior are most of them prophetical: not only describing, and as it were painting things moral and spiritual, but predicting also the future operation and effects of his gospel in the world.

As the husbandman forecasts in his mind the harvest to be expected from the nature of the seed and of the soil in which it is sown; or as the wise statesman foresees the effects of a political institution, according to the genius, principles, customs, and manners of the people; so with a more than human prescience our Lord foresaw and foretold the success of the Christian religion.

PARTICULARLY, the comparisons in the text were intended to describe the increase and progress of Christianity from a small beginning to its utmost extent and grandeur. And the propriety of the allusions and truth of the predictions have been already proved from the event; and we hope will be yet more illustriously verified in future ages. The kingdom of our Savior has spread already over a considerable part of the

the world, and among the moſt populous civilized and learned nations. And tho' the *Jews*, his own heritage, rejected him, and would not that he ſhould reign over them; yet the heathen have become his inheritance, and the uttermoſt parts of the earth his poſſeſſion. His religion ſoon ſpread beyond the narrow precinct of the *Jewiſh* territory and the *moſaic* inſtitution: It hath extended itſelf from ſea to ſea, and from the riſing of the ſun unto the going down thereof.

To this greatneſs and amplitude did the kingdom of heaven ariſe from the ſmalleſt origin. The founder of this extenſive empire was in appearance one of the meaneſt of the ſons of men; who, till the commencement of his miniſtry, ſcarcely diſtinguiſhed himſelf from the reſt of mankind, even of the loweſt rank: And after he entered upon his great office, continued to bear the external marks of poverty and meanneſs; and in the ſhort ſpace of four years

years was apprehended, condemned, and put to an ignominious death, as a public malefactor. His disciples also, by whose instrumentality he was to accomplish his design, and build up his intended empire, were persons of the like rank, and of themselves utterly incapable of so great an enterprize. His doctrine was not calculated to conciliate men by their worldly interests; nor his discourses, or manner of address, adapted to engage the passions of men in his favor. Yet this obscure person, by instruments so mean and weak, in so short a space of time, and in opposition to the passions, prejudices, and worldly interests of men, laid the foundation of a spiritual kingdom, which afterwards grew and prevailed, and which we believe shall at last spread into an universal empire.

These circumstances of the commencement of our holy religion, the low state and ignominious sufferings of our Savior and his apostles, and the singularity of their

their doctrine and institution, made their success, in the natural course of things, very improbable; and in fact, they were at first a great impediment to its rise, and raised a violent and lasting opposition to it. *Many,* say the evangelists, *were offended at him;* at the poverty of his appearance, the place of his birth, and of his residence, and the nature of his discourses. They said, *Is he not the son of a carpenter?—Can any good come out of Nazareth?—Doth any prophet arise out of Galilee?*—That *he spake like a Samaritan* — and *one who had a devil* — That many of his discourses were *hard sayings,* unintelligible, or seemingly absurd, being contrary to their established opinions. Hence the gospel became, as the apostle expresses it, to the *Jews a stumbling-block, and to the Greeks foolishness.* But these circumstances are now to us matter of glory, and not of offence; and afford to every impartial and attentive person a strong evidence of the divinity of our religion. Hence *Jesus Christ* appears to us, as the *power of God* and the *wisdom of God:* and his gospel, not a scheme of human policy, or a *cunningly-devised fable,* not the offspring of chance, or the product of wild fancy and enthusiastic invention; but a revelation from heaven, the truth and the grace of GOD appearing to mankind.

This divine procedure is not to be thought dissimilar to other operations of the power and providence of GOD in the material world, or in the course of human affairs. Do we not often see great and wonderful effects proceeding from causes either unknown, or that appear obscure and inadequate? Is not the general process of nature of this kind? Are not the ordinary and continual operations in it, carried on by instruments and materials, which seem to every vulgar eye slight and trivial? Do not the plants of the earth, (according to our Savior's own comparison) which grow to a great magnitude and height, and put forth large branches,

spring

spring from small seeds, some hardly perceptible to human sense? And do we not derive from the common dirt of the earth, and from the most vile and loathsome materials, all that admirable variety and profusion of beauty, which we behold on the face of things, and the whole support of human life?—And in the affairs of mankind, have not the greatest events often depended on very minute ones? the most wonderful revolutions been wrought by mean agents? and the most extensive and beneficial effects flowed from causes seemingly despicable and improbable?——The elevation of *David* from the state of a shepherd to fill the throne of *Israel*, to make that nation victorious over their enemies, and to establish the law and worship of God in it—The rise of the patriarch *Joseph* from the condition of a slave and prisoner, to be chief over the kingdom of Egypt; and the great revolutions that followed in consequence of his being sold by his brethren — may be recited as instances of this kind; befide many other both from facred and profane hiftory. And to refer to a well-known modern hiftory, who that beheld a perfon in a mean habit, laboring in the daily employment of a carpenter, would at firft view have imagined, that this was a ftep towards the accomplifhment of one of the greateft and moft beneficial defigns that have been conceived by human wifdom and policy, which that perfon fo mean in appearance was then meditating, and in effect executing?—Moreover, is it not juftly confidered, as a proof of the higheft wifdom, to operate in the fimpleft manner; to bring to pafs great affairs by little means; to draw from diftant obfcure caufes, effects of manifeft and extenfive utility, and to rife from the loweft beginning to the fublimeft end?—And, as the wifdom of GOD, or, (to ufe the language of the apoftle) as the foolifhnefs of GOD excels the wifdom of men, and the weaknefs of GOD furpaffes the power of men; fo much more excellent and wonderful are his operations. And as in the material univerfe, he produceth

duceth all the various and astonishing effects in nature by obscure and latent causes; so in the intellectual world, he executes designs of immense extent, the purposes of his unerring counsel and perfect goodness, by mysterious ways and means, by causes and instruments which may seem little and contemptible, or which may be indiscernable to our narrow sight, till by seeing the great and manifest effects, we are led to trace out the several steps, and explore the hidden and remote causes.

When our blessed Savior was cut off in the midst of his days, in so short a time after his public appearance in the world, and with such circumstances of ignominy and misery, when *his disciples all forsook him and fled*, lay hid in corners, and said one to another in despair, " *We trusted it was he* " *who should have redeemed Israel*, but our " hopes are now at an end," (his crucifixion confounding all their conceptions and expectations of him :) Then the seed of of the gospel seemed to die and perish, and our Lord's design was in all human probability rendered abortive. Yet immediately afterward it took root in the earth, and sprung up with a surprizing celerity of growth. The gospel made a rapid progress into different parts of the world: and the vast success of it in that age was owing, not to the persuasive words of eloquence, or the devices of human art and wit; but to the miraculous *demonstration of the Spirit and power of God* which accompanied it.

AT the end of the apostolic age, when the miraculous gifts of the Holy Spirit were withdrawn, and Christianity was left to stand by its own internal strength, and when the secular powers of the world were bent upon its destruction; then again, according to human conjecture and foresight, it must have declined and sunk to nothing. Nevertheless it still increased, and diffused itself in so gradual and imperceptible a manner, as to demonstrate the truth and propriety

propriety of another prophetic comparison of our Savior: *So is the kingdom of God, as if a man should cast seed into the ground, and should sleep and rise night and day, and the seed should spring and grow up he knoweth not how.*—Thus by indiscernable steps and degrees it encreased; till in the time of the emperor *Constantine*, it was spread into all parts of the known world; and in the compass of a few reigns afterwards became the public religion universally professed throughout the *Roman* empire, Paganism as well as *Judaism* sinking and vanishing before it.

AFTER that period, instead of encreasing and flourishing yet more in the world, it declined both in extent, and in its power and influence upon the minds of men, and was a third time reduced to an imminent danger of being entirely subverted, and a counterfeit religion and most detestable form of tyranny substituted in its stead. This deplorable change might be thought

at

at first view contrary to all probable expectation; since it had then those secular advantages on its side, which were before employed against it: and it was owing in fact, not so much to any foreign force or outward violence, as to an inward corruption. The celestial plant of the gospel had endured the storms of adversity and persecution; and though they threatened its utter extirpation, took deeper root and sprung up. But when these tempests were overblown, it became subject to another danger, equally or more to be dreaded, an internal distemper and decay. In this respect it resembled the civil states and kingdoms of the world; which are in general more hurt and endangered by intestine corruption and discord, than by foreign invasions. So a train of internal disorders introduced and propagated not by open but secret and domestic enemies became more detrimental to this spiritual state than any external opposition. Wide breaches were made upon its constitution, its fundamental

damental laws were dispensed with and almost annulled, its institutions perverted, and its principles changed; intestine factions and discords were set on foot and fomented, the ministers and public defenders of it became themselves disaffected and betrayers of its laws and privileges: it was abused to the worst purposes of temporal power and sacerdotal dominion. Hence, instead of a state of the greatest freedom and virtue, it degenerated into the most abject slavery and wickedness, and was changed from a spiritual and divine government into the worst kind of worldly tyrannies under the worst of men. An astonishing scene to review! such as might tempt us (as it has in fact tempted some) to call in question the genuineness and authority of the Christian religion; if we did not find this very corruption and tyranny predicted in the writings of the New Testament, even in terms so clear and expressive, that a more just and comprehensive

prehensive description cannot be given of it since the event.

When that great apostacy and the causes of it are duly considered, it cannot be thought unaccountable that Christianity hath lost ground, or been so ineffectual to the purpose of reforming the world; or that Mahometanism, which cut off some gross absurdities prevalent amongst Christians should spread to a wide extent: or that the Jews should persist in their infidelity: or that an unconquerable prejudice should remain in all the unbelieving nations against the reception of the Christian institution so adulterated and deformed. The church of *Rome* hath indeed labored abundantly to propagate her spurious system of Christianity throughout the world, hath employed vast numbers of missionaries or mock-apostles, and appointed large funds for that purpose; but hitherto with not much success; their boasted multitudes of converts being for the most part either fictitious

tious or merely nominal. And it is no breach of Christian piety to wish they may never have more success; nor any presumption to predict they never will.

How speedy and wonderful a progress did the kingdom of heaven make, from the smallest beginning till it overspread the Roman empire!—And it rose, not only unassisted, but opposed by the powers of this world both temporal and spiritual; as the apostle describes it in his epistle to the Ephesians: *We wrestle not only with flesh and blood, i. e.* the common infirmities and prejudices of human nature; *but with powers and authorities, with rulers of the darkness of this world, with spiritual wickednesses in heavenly things, i. e.* with the secular and ecclesiastical powers of judaism and heathenism. But the kingdom of antichrist, though the propagation of it hath been attempted by employing immense military forces, as in the holy war, and by all the negociations and artifices of human policy,

policy, and by innumerable miſſions ſupported by vaſt funds, yet hath not been able to extend its power over any one infidel nation. So different was the ſucceſs of the true Chriſtian religion carrying rational conviction along with it, and tending ſolely to the benefit of mankind, and of the counterfeit papal religion operating by fraud and force, and intended only to enſlave the world.

YET during this long period of corruption, Chriſtianity ſtill had its root alive in the earth, tho' the branches were blaſted and withered, and tho' many foreign plants had been grafted upon it, producing bitter and poiſonous fruits. When learning and the ſtudy of the holy Scriptures were revived among Chriſtians; when they turned their attention to the doctrines of our Savior and his apoſtles, and began to learn from their words, what the Chriſtian religion truly was in its original inſtitution, and to diſcover how groſsly it had been miſtaken

mistaken and perverted; many learned and excellent men exerted themselves with great activity and industry to correct such enormous abuses, and to promote a general reformation. Hence Christianity hath gradually revived, and in some degree regained its primitive vigor and spirit; and extended itself in the world, though in the midst of much confusion, many enemies and great discouragements: whilst professed unbelievers have opposed it on the one side, and the abettors of the antichristian corruptions, with greater enmity and fury, on the other. But notwithstanding all such opposition, so long as men continue to pay their chiefest attention and reverence to the discourses of our Savior himself, and to derive their religion from him, as from the fountain-head; Christianity will continue to spring up and encrease, and produce the noble fruits of freedom, virtue, and happiness. Unbelievers themselves will in time be convinced, that the restoration of genuine Christianity is the only effectual remedy for thofe corruptions and oppreffions in the Chriftian world, againft which they have fo loudly exclaimed, and which have raifed in their minds a moft unjuft prejudice againft the gofpel. Nothing can be more directly oppofite to fuch evils than the very doctrine and authority of our Savior himfelf. To weaken the influence, therefore, of that doctrine and authority upon the minds of men, will be found in effect, not to guard them againft, but to expofe them to the influence of religious delufion, of erroneous opinions, and fuperftitious ceremonies. But the world muft firft be purged from the corruptions of antichriftianifm, before true Chriftianity can flourifh and obtain a general reception and influence. The Chriftian world will, we hope, in time, become univerfally reformed; and then our holy religion will acquire in fome meafure the honor and fuccefs due to its intrinfic excellence and merit; and the unbelieving nations become difpofed to a reception and belief of it. Then the prophetical

tical descriptions in the text will be accomplished, in a more compleat and adequate manner, than has hitherto appeared. That divine plant which took its rise from the smallest *seed* will become *the greatest of herbs,* and grow up into a *tree,* so large, *that the birds of the air may come and lodge in the branches of it.* That spirit which our Savior infused into the minds of his disciples, and which gradually spread like *leaven* in the first ages of Christianity, will again diffuse itself, till the *whole mass is fermented by it.*

THE prophecies of the New Testament plainly declare, that a general apostacy and corruption would ensue at the coming of antichrist: that this would obstruct the advancement of Christianity: and that antichristianism must be destroyed, and a general reformation take place, before the Jews will be converted, or the fulness of the Gentiles come in: that then the church of Christ will flourish and the gospel spread throughout

throughout the world. When the Christian world shall become a scene of virtue, knowledge, freedom, and concord, and the gospel is seen to have beneficial effects on human society; then will Christianity recommend itself to all men, appear excellent in the eyes even of infidels, and the propagation of it become practicable and easy: then we may expect all the predictions concerning the extent and grandeur of the kingdom of heaven in this world, to receive their fullest accomplishment, and according to the words of our Savior, *That every plant which his heavenly Father hath not planted shall be plucked up*, every false religion be abolished, and his religion become universal.

We have considered our Savior as denoting in these parables, by the expression of the *kingdom of heaven*, the state of Christianity on earth: yet it is certain, that he frequently denotes by the same expression the future state of mankind in the world to to come. In order then to remove all seeming inconsistency or ambiguity, we should attend to the connexion and resemblance between the present state of men, as governed by the gospel of our Savior, with their future state in another world. For it is in reality one and the same government, in its nature and effects, the government of reason and true religion, of the precepts of universal and eternal righteousness and goodness, or of the will of God as promulgated, enforced, and executed by our blessed Savior. Both constitutions have the same sovereign and the same laws; how much soever the scene and circumstances may be changed, or the privileges of the subject enlarged. He rules in the hearts of all faithful Christians at present, by means of his gospel published on earth; and will hereafter judge and reward them according to the same gospel. The immutable laws of truth, virtue, and goodness, which he requires his followers to observe in this life, constitute the very foundation and frame of that celeftial empire over all mankind which he has obtained, and which he is continually promoting and eftablifhing in another world. His kingdom then has an imperfect commencement in this life: And as far as the belief and practice of Chriftianity extend, there is fo far a veftige or fpecimen of his invifible and eternal kingdom; but mixed, in this world, with all thofe *evils and offences*, and thofe *workers of iniquity*, which, in the other, he will utterly extirpate. For it is not till after death and the refurrection that mankind become fubject to his imperial jurifdiction, and liable to be rewarded or punifhed by him according to their actions in this life. In one fenfe he is Lord of the *living*, as well as of the dead; as all men who know and believe his gofpel are bound to yield obedience to him: but the fanctions of his laws are not executed here: and in refpect to the exertion of his regal and judicial power,

power, *his kingdom* (as he told the Roman governor) *is not of this world.*

THAT the comparisons in the text relate to the rise and growth of Christianity in this world, seems very evident. Whether they were at all intended, or can with any propriety be applied, so as to represent the rise and increase of the kingdom of heaven in another world, or the future state of mankind, is matter of mere doubtful conjecture. It may be, that the constitution of things hereafter will have a nearer resemblance, in some respects, to the state of things on earth, than human imagination is apt to suppose. But how much soever it may differ, or excel, in the most important respects; we are taught by our Savior and his apostles to form our ideas of the administration of *that kingdom of heaven* from the execution of human justice, and the establishment of order in the kingdoms of this world. As malefactors who are judged unworthy of the protection of society are here cut off and destroyed; as all good subjects are or ought to be preserved, and the worthy promoted; so shall it be in the future state, in a measure and degree far excelling the wisdom and justice of any human government, namely, in proportion to the deserts of every individual. And it is reasonable to apprehend, that the kingdom of heaven in the other world is a *progressive* state also; is making a gradual and continual advancement towards its utmost extent of dominion, perfection of order, and fulness of glory and felicity: this gradual process being similar to all the divine operations discernible in the creation around us.

Let us then consider ourselves, not only as subjects of a temporal kingdom, and bound by civil laws and obligations to serve the interests of that state to which we belong, and to be faithful to its constitution and sovereign; but as subjects of a higher government and members of a more extensive

extensive community, and bound by peculiar and eternal obligations to preserve inviolably this divine constitution, and bear a true allegiance to its invisible sovereign. The strongest arguments that can operate on human nature conspire in exciting our utmost endeavors to promote the peace, power, and enlargement of this kingdom of heaven. Here centers every generous sentiment, worthy design, and pious motive, that can affect the heart, or guide the actions of a rational creature and real Christian. No one who sincerely professeth Christianity can think himself unconcerned to rescue it from corruption and violation, and to restore and extend its influence. Let every one act according to his station as a good member of the Christian church and faithful subject of the kingdom of heaven. *All members have not the same office; yet we being many are one body in Christ, and every one members one of another.* Let each discharge his office according to the nature of it, and the obligations

gations of a Christian. *He that ministreth, let him wait on his ministering; he that teacheth, on teaching; he that exhorteth, on exhortation: he that giveth, let him do it with simplicity; he that ruleth, with diligence; he that sheweth mercy, with cheerfulness.* Above all, let every one order his own conversation as becometh the gospel of Christ: for there is nothing so vain and absurd, as to pretend a zeal for religion and the public interest of Christianity, and at the same time to disgrace and disserve it by a scandalous example. Nor let that antichristian imagination ever enter into our minds, that we can defend and advance the Christian cause by any methods of fraud, violence, or uncharitableness; but by those means alone, which the wisdom of the serpent joined to the innocence of the dove may suggest.

Let us not take alarm at little or imaginary dangers to the Christian religion, while we are not perhaps sufficiently aware of of those which are real and great. The most formidable danger is from an internal corruption, not an external opposition. It is that which gives all the ground of advantage, and furnishes all the weapons to the open adversaries of Christianity. If some men of rash tempers and superficial understandings, who have never taken pains to distinguish the dross from the gold, and to understand the nature of our religion, have taken occasion to reflect on Christianity, or to depreciate its ministry and worship, this consequence ought not to give us so much disturbance, as the cause, from which this evil of infidelity, and many others, have proceeded: for they can never fall into contempt, if not abused and corrupted. Their own intrinsic excellence and importance are a sufficient security. All groundless censures and contemptuous expressions, whether ludicrous or serious, will be found experimentally to have little effect; and are sufficiently refuted and best answered,

answered, by being easily overlooked and silently despised. We may safely trust to the common sense of mankind, and the natural force of truth; or if not to those, to the providence of God and the predictions of the New Testament; that infidelity shall never prevail against Christianity; and that the kingdom of heaven, when restored to its native soundness and vigor, and established on its own foundation, will support itself, increase in power and magnitude, and finally triumph over every false religion.

Here then let us fix our attention and employ our zeal and assiduity,—to heal the distempers of the Christian church, and restore our holy religion to its pristine health and natural strength; that so it may flourish and extend its salutary influence, enmity and opposition cease, knowledge be encreased, and the everlasting gospel successfully preached and propagated amongst

mongst all nations; till all the kingdoms of the world shall be united in the universal kingdom of our Lord and Savior *Jesus Christ*. Which God of his infinite mercy grant, through *Jesus Christ* our Lord.

PART II.

On the Parables in the fifteenth and sixteenth Chapters of St. LUKE.

ALL these parables, like the former, seem to have been spoke on the same day, and to the same audience. By considering them in this view, they appear, methinks, more intelligible and significant. They are moral paintings, in which our Savior exhibits the character, disposition,

and

and conduct of himself and the several parties of his audience, at the time he was speaking to them, and in reference to the censures his enemies were then throwing out against him. The description therefore is less extensive, but more particular and defined, than in those of the former part.

DISCOURSE I.

The Occasion of the following Parables.

Luke xv. 1, 2.

Then drew nigh to him all the publicans and sinners for to hear him. And the pharisees and scribes murmured, saying, This man receiveth sinners, and eateth with them.

THE best conduct of the wisest persons, instead of securing to them the esteem which they deserve, is often turned into matter of censure, being mistaken by the ignorant and misrepresented by the prejudiced. Was an angel from heaven to appear incarnate, and converse among men; not all his wisdom and virtue, exhibited as perfectly as the human state can admit, would exempt him from envy and hatred, nor consequently from reproach and calumny: And the more distinguished the character

character which he appeared to assume, the more would his words and actions be misinterpreted. The very superiority of his wisdom and goodness would give offence; to the ignorant, by surpassing their comprehension, and to the envious, by excelling their merit.—We shall not wonder at this, if we are duly apprized, how much the works and designs of the supreme all-wise Being himself have been villifyed, not only by the enemies, but also by some professed friends of religion: who have asserted, contrary to plain fact, that this world (though undoubtedly the work of GOD) is no better than a scene of disorder, deformity and misery, in which the evil far exceeds the good: and not contented with this, have supposed, that in another world, the greater part of mankind shall be preserved in a state of aggravated wickedness and misery to eternity; and consequently that the state of things shall be worse upon the whole than in this world.—If a scheme and purpose resembling this, which some men

men ascribe to the sovereign ruler of the universe, was to be imputed to any prince or governor on earth; would he not reject it with abhorrence as the blackest calumny, invented with a design to render himself and his government odious to his subjects? If then any men have taken such outrageous liberties with that Being, whom all men style the wisest and best, as to describe the present system of his works, and the future eternal scheme of his providence, in colors so dark and deformed; we cannot wonder, that any other eminent character should suffer reproach, from human mistakes and misrepresentations. For, as our *Savior* justly argues with his disciples, when he was going to send them abroad into the world, and foretold the reception they would meet with, and the hatred and contumely they would incur;—*The disciple is not above his master, nor the servant above his Lord. If they have called the master of the house Beelzebub; how much more will they call them of his houshold?*—If they loaded him with calumnies, his disciples could

have

have little reaſon to hope that they ſhould eſcape cenſure and abuſe. So, if the all-perfect Being is blaſphemed among men, and his actions are ſometimes not only miſ-underſtood, but perverted in the opinions of men to the worſt purpoſes; it is not a matter of aſtoniſhment, if the Son of God alſo ſuffered unjuſt reproach. It is indeed acknowledged, that perſons of wiſdom, probity, and virtue, have a natural claim to the eſteem of mankind, and generally obtain it. But when theſe qualities are exerted in an extraordinary degree, and in oppoſition to men's prejudices, or pride, or ſelfiſh paſſions and deſigns; then even innocence is thought an offence, virtue odious, and wiſdom oppreſſive, by thoſe who imagine themſelves to be injured, or oppoſed, or eclipſed by them. Nay, tho' a beneficent and miraculous power ſhould be added, giving the higheſt authority; yet ſuch men, to evade conviction, will impute that power to the devil rather than to God.—All this was verified in the inſtance

stance of our Savior. While he remained in obscurity, and concealed his wisdom, goodness, and power from the notice of the public, he lived free from enmity and reproach. But when he discovered himself, and the fame of his miracles drew multitudes after him; when he began to instruct and reform the people, and to proclaim the kingdom of heaven; then hatred and opposition began, and increased also, in proportion to the increase of his fame, and the larger displays of his superior endowments. Then he had to sustain the contradiction of sinners, the detraction of slanderers, the derision of fools, the contempt of the proud, and the vengeance of the powerful.

We shall pass by all the contemptuous and malicious reflections thrown out against him on account of his parentage, relations, country, and place of residence. His enemies were not content with calling up every external circumstance, which might

The occasion of the following Parables.

might contribute, as they imagined, to depreciate his character; nor with putting his wisdom to the proof, by artful and insidious questions; nor with ascribing his miracles, when they could no longer dispute the reality of them, to a diabolic power;—but they openly and directly charged him with impiety, blasphemy, and immorality, and the worst construction was put upon every part of his conduct.— We shall select one part of it for our present consideration, which will lead us to the passage recorded in the text.

FROM the time of his entring upon his public office, he admitted all persons who resorted to him, accepted invitations from them, and freely conversed with people of low rank and mean characters, such as were known among the *Jews* by the opprobrious names of *publicans* and *sinners*. This conduct gave a handle to the *scribes* and *pharisees* of defaming him, which they seem to have laid hold of with eagerness.

To

To this end they represented him as no better than a companion of libertines and profligates, and addicted like them to intemperance and excess. *Behold, they said, a glutton and a wine-bibber, a friend of publicans and sinners.* Possibly they might be sincerely of an opinion that his conduct was inconsistent with piety and sanctity. For as they were great pretenders to religion, they thought themselves too holy, and were in reality too proud, to be seen in such company. They would have thought themselves defiled by sitting at the same table with a publican. Our Savior has given us a remarkable specimen of the language and spirit of one of them, as expressed in an act of devotion: *God, I thank thee, that I am not as other men are,— or even as this publican.* To associate, therefore, in any manner with such persons, appeared to them incompatible with a religious character, and most of all with that of the *Messiah*. They drew from hence an unanswerable argument, as they thought, against

against him: At least they were willing to make the largest use of it, both by reflecting upon him in his absence, and reviling him in his presence.

We find three several occasions mentioned by the *evangelists* on which he vindicated his own conduct in this particular.——*John the Baptist*, saith he, *came neither eating nor drinking:* i. e. he lived in the wilderness, assumed an austerity of manners, and appeared as a person mortified to the world and all its entertainments. On the contrary, *the Son of man came eating and drinking*—frequented cities and places of the greatest concourse, accepted of entertainments, made use of the common provisions of life, and freely conversed with all sorts of persons. One would imagine then, that they, who had censured the rigid manners of *John the Baptist*, would approve the contrary deportment of our *Savior*. But neither method pleased them: they were determined to find fault. The

The former they said was *mad* and possessed by some evil *demon*; and the latter addicted to intemperance, and *a friend of publicans and sinners.* Hence he compares them to perverse and froward *children*, who would always reject what their companions proposed; and on every occasion, whether grave or pleasant, show the contrary temper. *But wisdom,* he adds, *is justified of all her children.* All wise and impartial persons would see and acknowledge a propriety and rectitude of conduct in both instances, as suited to the difference of situation, character, and design in each. *John* the *Baptist* had no power of working miracles: It was therefore requisite to his design, that he should exhibit some other extraordinary qualities, in order to draw attention and respect. And it has been found in all ages, that such appearances of austerity have been most effectual to engage the attention and esteem of the multitude. But our *Savior* had a miraculous power, and gave many amazing proofs

proofs of it. This then was a mark of diftinction fufficient to point him out to the people, and to draw multitudes after him. His virtue, therefore, was of the moft humane and focial kind, adapted to civil life, and to the natural condition and common affairs of mankind. He neither wanted nor defired to draw men's attention, or excite their veneration, by any other fingularity of appearance and behavior, than by his perfect innocence and goodnefs, added to the wifdom of his inftructions and the power of his miracles. If then the fcribes and pharifees had not been prepoffeffed by the worft prejudices; inftead of cenfuring, they would have admired a behavior fo natural and humane, and fo remote from all oftentation. But men may be of fo perverfe a temper, that nothing will pleafe them: freedom and referve, ferioufnefs and cheerfulnefs will be alike offenfive: the more you endeavor to oblige them, the further you are from it. The evil difpofition which they harbor in
their

their own minds, they impute to every perfon around them, and moft of all to thofe who by merit have raifed their envy and malice. It was not poffible then, that our bleffed Savior could avoid the reproach of men fo ill-difpofed. For the more excellent his life and converfation, and the more humanity and goodnefs he difcovered to the people, the more he offended their pride and excited their difguft: Infomuch that when he had miraculoufly healed a poor woman of an inveterate diftemper on the Sabbath-day, they took occafion to charge him with a breach of the fourth commandment. This inftance plainly demonftrates the badnefs of their fpirit, the perfect innocence of his conduct, and the truth of the miracle. For certainly, if they could have found any other objection, either to the reality of the miracle, or the rectitude of his conduct, they never would have thought of fo abfurd an accufation; and inftead of applauding him for fo wonderful an act of goodnefs and charity, have

reproached

reproached him as a breaker of the Sabbath. These hypocrites concealed their malice under a cloke of religion and a veneration for the Sabbath-day. With what propriety and force of reason does he refute this charge, in his answer to the ruler of the synagogue, who told the people in a passion;—that there were six days in the week in which they might come and be healed, and that they ought not to come on the Sabbath-day. *Thou hypocrite, doth not every one of you think it right to loose his ox or his ass and lead him to the water on the Sabbath-day? And ought not this woman, a daughter of Abraham, to be loosed on that day from the bond of her infirmity, in which she hath been bound lo these eighteen years?*

On another occasion he makes a further reply to the charge of his associating with publicans and sinners: *The whole*, saith he, *have no need of the physician, but the sick. I came to call, not the righteous, but sinners to repentance.*—The reason contained in these words

words is clear and cogent. If our Savior came to heal the diftempered minds of men, and his proper character was that of an inftructor and reformer; muft he avoid the company of thofe who moft of all needed inftruction, when they offered themfelves to him, and were willing to give attention?—Would not this have been as inconfiftent, as if a phyfician fhould give advice to perfons in health only, and refufe to vifit the fick and difeafed, who have the greateft need of his affiftance?—If the fcribes and pharifees were fo wife and righteous as they pretended to be; they had fo much the lefs occafion for advice or room for amendment. He taught the doctrine of repentance, in order to forgivenefs and falvation: and to whom could he fo properly addrefs his difcourfe, as to finners, who confeffedly ftood in fo abfolute need of it?—*But a juft man*, he afferts, *needeth no repentance*. For though no perfon can be fo righteous, as to have no errors or failings, or no room to make a further proficiency;

proficiency; yet it is said with an exact propriety, that *a just man needeth no repentance:* because, in the full and proper sense, repentance is a conversion, not from a good life to a better, but from a wicked life to a good one—or a change, not from one degree of virtue and goodness to another, but from evil to good, from vice to virtue. It supposes a person to have lived in a course of wickedness, or to have committed some heinous crime. But no man can be said to repent of a vice he hath not been guilty of, or of a crime which he hath never committed. Indeed, every good man will be sorry for any incidental failures or deviations in any part of his conduct, and will endeavor to guard against them for the future. But this is more properly styled perseverance, or growth and improvement in goodness, than repentance, which implies a change of mind; whereas the very definition of a righteous man, is one whose mind or purpose is to do that which is right: and therefore,

therefore, though he may happen to commit a fault, or be involved in an error, for which he will blame himself; yet there is upon the whole no change of mind, or of his habitual difpofition: all that is requifite is, that his mind return to itfelf, or to its own prevailing principles and refolutions. But finners have need of repentance, and want to be *renewed in the inward man,* as the Apoftle expreffes it: *i. e.* new fentiments and difpofitions muft be acquired; and they muft learn to think and act with fuch views and motives as they have not been accuftomed to. Their minds labor under fome diftemper which requires powerful remedies. To fuch perfons as thefe the Savior of the world chiefly applied, calling them to repentance, and intending by his divine fkill to heal their internal difeafes, and to produce a moft important and happy change in their minds. Had the fcribes and pharifees objected to this part of his conduct, only becaufe they were defirous of having all the benefit of his converſation to themſelves; or becauſe they thought thoſe ſinners incapable of amendment, or not ſo well diſpoſed as themſelves to receive advantage from his inſtructions; their error might have been excuſable. But it is evident that this was far from their intention. Some of that denomination were indeed of a different character: but moſt of them not only thought themſelves too wiſe and too good, to receive inſtruction from him; but derided and inſulted him, and endeavored by all means to deſtroy his character and influence.—— For inſtance—after they had ſtrictly examined the man who was born blind, and his parents alſo, concerning the fact of his receiving ſight, and they could lay hold of no pretence to deny the reality of the miracle; yet they ſaid to the man, *Give thanks to God: for as to this man* (Jeſus) *we know that he is a ſinner.* They were determined at all events to pronounce him a wicked man. This appeared very ſtrange to the poor man who had been cured; and who,

who, touched with gratitude for the great bleſſing he had received, and judging according to his own natural reaſon, vindicates the character of his benefactor in oppoſition to the opinion and authority of theſe great men. He uſes an argument very clear and convincing, *viz.* that GOD would not impower a wicked man to work miracles in order to carry on his evil deſigns. For indeed, if we cannot reſt aſſured of this, that GOD will not ſuffer *the ſeal of heaven*, the ſtamp of real miracles, to be put to falſehood and wickedneſs; how much would it weaken, if not ſubvert the very foundation of all faith and confidence in him?—But the argument has a peculiar force in this inſtance. For if Jeſus was not only endowed with ſuch an aſtoniſhing power as to work this miracle, but ſhewed ſo much goodneſs and humility, as to ſingle out a poor blind beggar for his object, who could make him no recompence, and from whom he could not expect to gain ſo much reputation

tation and applause, as from a person of rank and distinction; it must be very unnatural to suppose, that he was at the same time a wicked person, carrying on some fradulent and unjust design. It is evident then, that the aforementioned persons were actuated by a spirit of malevolence, and sought to charge upon him the guilt and blame of their own wickedness. When he makes, therefore, this reply to them, that *the whole have no need of a physician, but the sick:* and that he *came to call, not the righteous, but sinners to repentance:*—he does not mean to allow, that they were righteous men; but only that the publicans and sinners were proper objects of his kind instructions: as they not only discovered a willingness to hear him, but in the opinion of the pharisees themselves, stood in the greatest need of repentance. He perfectly understood the true disposition and character of the former party as well as the latter: and therefore, in the 5th of Matthew, assures his disciples, that if their

righteousness

righteousness did not exceed the righteousness of the scribes and pharisees, they should by no means enter into the kingdom of heaven:—— a declaration surprizing to the multitude. For these men were in appearance and by reputation the most holy and religious. They were rulers of the synagogue, rabbies, doctors, masters, and fathers in Israel, who fasted twice in the week, paid tythes of all that they possessed, wore holy garments, distributed alms by sound of trumpet, disfigured their faces, and made long prayers: yet notwithstanding these affected appearances, he who penetrated their hearts knew them to be hypocrites, and to be more wicked and incorrigible than the publicans and sinners, whom they affected to treat with the utmost contempt; and seemed to think it a deep blot upon our Lord's character, that he vouchsafed to hold any conversation with them.

WE have now considered two replies on different occasions, by which he vindicates this

this part of his own conduct.—A third occasion we find in the words of the text. *Then drew near to him all the publicans and sinners to hear him. But the pharisees and scribes murmured, saying, This man receiveth sinners and eateth with them.* Upon which he once more condescends to vindicate himself, in opposition to this invidious censure. This he does in so ample, so admirable, and so instructive a manner, that we shall find a subject, not only of curiosity, but if it be not our own fault, of great advantage and improvement; if we give a proper attention to the following parables of this chapter, which appear to have been one continued speech in answer to the afore-mentioned charge.

But we refer the consideration of them to the following discourses.—In the mean time, let us us take a view of a very instructive spectacle, and retain the impression of it in our minds.

SEE

SEE the wisest and best person who ever appeared among men—behold the great prophet of GOD and Savior of the world cloathed with perfect humanity, seated amidst a concourse of men of different ranks and characters, not exclusive of the meanest, addressing himself to them with inimitable wisdom and propriety, laying hold of every question and incident for an occasion of insinuating the sentiments of knowledge and virtue into their minds, of exciting their thinking powers, assisting their feeble reason, and healing their mental diseases. And when we read and consider his discourses, let us observe his charity and condescension to the publicans and sinners, his candor in respect to their ignorance and vices, his sincere desire of their amendment and happiness; his serenity and magnanimity in bearing the disgrace his enemies endeavored to throw upon him, and the fertility of invention and force of reason, by which, in so many different replies, he anfwers their objections, and refutes their calumnies.

Let us hence learn to pay more attention to his moft excellent inftructions. Let us never imagine ourfelves too wife to be taught, or too good to be amended; nor defpife any whom we may fuppofe to be deftitute of our attainments. Let us beware of the *pharifaic* fpirit and language, faying to our neighbor, *Stand off, I am holier than thou.* Let us guard againft pride and felf-flattery, in eftimating our own worth,—and infolence and cenforioufnefs in refpect to others;—and imitate to the utmoft of our power the perfect humanity and goodnefs of our bleffed Savior.

DISCOURSE II.

Of the careful Shepherd.

LUKE XV, 3.—&c.

And he spake this parable unto them, saying, What man among you having an hundred sheep, if he lose one of them, doth not leave the ninety and nine in the wilderness, and go after that which is lost until he find it? And when he hath found it, he layeth it upon his shoulders rejoicing. And when he cometh home, he calleth together his friends and neighbors, saying unto them, Rejoice with me: for I have found my sheep which was lost. I say unto you, that likewise joy shall be in heaven over one sinner that repenteth, more than over ninety and nine just persons who need no repentance. Either what woman having ten pieces of silver, if she lose one piece, doth not light a candle, and sweep the house, and seek diligently till she find it? And when she hath found it, she calleth her friends and neighbors together, saying, Rejoice with me, for I found the piece which I had lost. Likewise I say unto you, there is joy in the presence of the angels of G O D *over one sinner that repenteth.*

WE have considered, in the preceeding discourse, the character and conduct of the *pharisees* and *scribes*, particularly, the envy and hatred which they conceived against our *Savior*, and the means which they made use of, to destroy his reputation and influence. He so far disappointed their expectations in the appearance he made, was so little disposed to flatter their pride, or fall in with their prejudices, taught the people such sentiments, and in a manner so superior to theirs, so freely reprehended the superstitions they taught, censured the impositions they practised, and exposed their fraud and hypocrisy; that their envy of his fame and merit,

merit, their averfion to his doctrine and character, their refentment of his procedure, and their malice againſt his perſon, were wrought to ſuch a height, that they were determined to ſeize the firſt opportunity of putting him to death: And at laſt, in full council, came to a reſolution, expreſſed by the high prieſt, *That it was expedient that one man ſhould die for the people, and not the whole nation periſh.* The true meaning of which was, that it was requiſite to their purpoſe, to take away his life, whether it could be done legally, or not.

But at firſt they were contented with endeavoring to blaſt his reputation, and to perſuade themſelves and others, by various pretences, that he had neither the wiſdom nor the ſanctity requiſite to the character of the *Meſſiah*. When they obſerved him, therefore, to be eaſy of acceſs to all ſorts of perſons, admitting *publicans and ſinners* into his preſence, fitting down to meat, holding converſation converfation with them, and delivering inftructions to them; they haftily concluded, that he acted inconfiftently with the virtue and holinefs of a *prophet*, efpecially of the *Meſſiah*; and took advantage of it, to infult and defame him.

We have already confidered two different anfwers, which our Savior gave to this charge, which his enemies made ufe of to his great difhonor, and full difproof (as they would reprefent it) of all the evidence he gave of his character and authority.—We fhall now proceed to the parables in this chapter, which were all fpoke in anfwer to the fame charge. But it may be proper firft to recall to mind, what fort of perfons our *Savior's* audience confifted of, and take into our view their different characters, fentiments, and difpofitions, connected with the circumftances of the occafion. This is the only method by which we can attain to a clear underftanding of our *Lord's* difcourfes. Without this,

this, men may comment upon his words, and twift them to a variety of meanings, till they expound away the true fenfe and fpirit, inftead of becoming able, either to explain them to others, or to underftand them for themfelves. For our Savior always fpeaks to the inmoft thoughts of his audience, and with a view to the ftate, character, and difpofitions of all around him. It is therefore by entering as far as poffible into the fame view, that we fhall perceive the wifdom, propriety, and utility of his difcourfes, underftand the principal defign in each of them, and learn to apply them properly to our own fituation and conduct in life.

The audience prefent when thefe parables were fpoke confifted of *three very different parties.*

(1.) The *fcribes* and *pharifees* who had cenfured him, and thereby given the occafion of thefe parables.——

(2.) The

(2.) The *publicans* and *sinners*, who reforted to him in a great number on purpose to hear him.———

(3.) His own *disciples*.

His intentions, therefore, were,

To confute the objections, and expose the ill temper of the first *party*———

To encourage the second in their good dispositions———

And to confirm the last in their respect and obedience.

The excellence of these parabolic discourses will appear in the clearest light, if we constantly keep in mind *these several intentions*.

In this parable he directed his speech to the first party: And his representation was proper to convey to their minds the most convincing argument in vindication of himself, and confutation of their cavils and objections, if they were open to conviction, and would assent to reason. For he points out

out to them in a clear and defined view, the propriety, humanity, and moral excellence of his own conduct.

(1.) THE propriety of it, as exactly agreeable to those ideas of prudence and fitness, which are common to mankind. For he acted in his spiritual capacity, as all men would be naturally disposed to act, in all similar concerns of a temporal nature. Every person in the world, who hath any possessions, which he puts a value upon, and thinks himself obliged to preserve, if he should happen to lose but a small part, his attention and diligence are immediately applyed to the recovery of that which he hath lost. This naturally becomes the first object of his concern: and his attention is much greater, for the time being, to that part which is lost, than to all that remains; and if he succeeds in his attempts to regain it, the recovery gives him more pleasure and joy, for the present, than the security of all his other possessions. This is perfectly

fectly natural, and according to the sense and experience of all persons in their civil and worldly affairs. So our *Savior*, in the affairs of religion, considering himself as related to the *Jewish* nation, having a spiritual property in it, and a concern for its reformation and welfare, applyed himself to bring the *publicans* and *sinners* to repentance; and in this acted in proper character, and fulfilled a part of his office. He was *the great shepherd of Israel*, and sought to recover, in the first place, *the lost sheep of the house of Israel*. It became him, as instructor, reformer, and *Savior*, to extend his generous care to them. Had he acted otherwise, and like the haughty *pharisee*, treated them with disregard and contempt, and excluded them from his presence, when they drew near to him on purpose to hear him; this would have been a conduct as improper and unnatural, as if the shepherd had suffered part of his flock to go astray and be lost, without using any endeavors to recover it; or the
woman

woman had neglected all search, in order to find the piece which she had lost.

We may observe here, that to heighten the figure, and add force to the argument, *our Lord* supposes the shepherd to have lost but *one* sheep out of an hundred, and the woman but *one* piece out of ten: yet on this supposition, it was usual and natural, that they should immediately think of recovering what they had lost, and use all proper means in order to that end. Now they who were denominated among the *Jews, publicans* and *sinners,* were a numerous part of the nation; and many of them were at this time in *our Lord*'s presence: There was therefore a more evident propriety and usefulness in his endeavoring to reclaim so many. But though his instructions had no greater effect than to reclaim *one* among them all; yet the recovery of that *one*, should in reason, and according to men's natural temper and way of thinking in all other affairs, be considered

dered as a valuable acquisition, and a proper occasion of joy.

(2.) He points out, not only the natural propriety of his conduct, but the moral fitness and goodness of it, as proceeding from a temper of humanity and benevolence, and a mind intent upon promoting the higheft welfare of mankind, and confequently rejoicing in every inftance of fuccefs in fo excellent a defign. Had the *scribes* and *pharifees* been poffeffed of the true fpirit of religion, the fpirit of candor and benevolence, or a defire of the reformation and happinefs of their fellow creatures; they would have been pleafed with every inftance of his fuccefs, and ready to rejoice with him, like the fhepherd's friends and neighbors, on account of his reclaiming thofe finners. Had but a tenth part of the *Jewifh* nation (according to the fecond reprefentation) or but the hundredth part (agreeably to the firft) confifted of profligate

profligate and reprobate perfons, and had all the reft been truly juft and good men; yet the *Savior* of the world would have thought it worthy of his attention, becoming his character, and agreeable to the higheft wifdom and humanity, to receive them with kindnefs, when they offered themfelves to him; and inftead of excluding them from his inftructions, to give them the ftrongeft encouragement to repentance. By turning this conduct into an occafion of reproach and infult, his adverfaries difcovered fuch a fpirit, as he thought fit to expofe to their own view: which he does, by reprefenting, with peculiar fimplicity and force, the natural, the proper, the humane, the celeftial difpofition upon the fame occafion—the *celeftial* difpofition:—For he afferts, that *there is joy in heaven*, or amongft *the angels, over one finner that repenteth*;—one of thofe defpifed publicans and finners, *more than over ninety and nine juft perfons* (fuch as the other party affumed to be) *who need no repentance.*—

This addition to the parable greatly enhances the spirit and force of the argument. As it is natural in men, how large soever their present possessions may be, and though they have lost but a small part in proportion to the whole, yet, to conceive a more immediate and sensible joy at the recovery of that small part, than in the possession of all the rest;—so our Savior ascribes the like quality to the nature of those superior Beings, who are styled the angels of GOD: who notwithstanding the vast extent of their respective provinces, and the inexhaustible fund of happiness they are always possessed of, yet are capable of receiving a particular and additional joy at every event which is agreeable to their sublime views and benevolent desires. And such is their benevolence, so far do they consider themselves as interested in the welfare of mankind, tho' an inferior species of creatures, that the virtue of good men is a continual object of their satisfaction; and at the same time, and for the

the same reason, the conversion of a sinner a particular occasion of joy to them. This beautiful image of celestial goodness and benevolence, even towards the lowest individual of the human species, was an admirable contrast to the deformity and malignity of temper in the scribes and pharisees. The *angels* were disposed to rejoice with him at his success in converting the publicans and sinners: but this was so far from being an occasion of joy to these *men*, that it excited their spleen and indignation. *There is joy in heaven over* one *sinner that repenteth:* but they had rather the whole generation of publicans and sinners should remain unconverted, than that his influence and authority should spread among the people.—He adds, *more than over ninety and nine just persons who need no repentance:*— But they looked upon themselves as being so righteous and religious, as to merit all our Savior's attention and respect; and that he ought to have paid no regard to persons so much inferior to them.

Now to make an application of the foregoing parable, to the several parties of our Savior's audience.—First, to the pharisees and scribes: the sum of the argument contained in these representations, and designed for their conviction, is briefly to this effect:—that if a *sheep*, or *a piece of coin*, be thought of value sufficient to employ men's care and diligence to recover them when lost; how much more *a human creature?*—For how much is a *man*, as he argues in another place, better than a *sheep?*—The meanest of the human species is certainly of more intrinsic value, than any part of that worldly property which men are so sollicitous to preserve. This is agreeable to the sense and judgment of superior Beings: they do not estimate the worth of things according to the proud and selfish conceits of men: they see no such difference, as men are apt to fancy, between the prince and the peasant, the pharisee and the publican: and so remote are they from that pride and insolence of temper which tempted

tempted the pharifees and fcribes to look upon their fellow-creatures with fo much difdain, that there is joy amongft them over one finner that repenteth.—Now let us only imagine to ourfelves the fupercilious and morofe countenance of the aforefaid party, upon their feeing the publicans and finners drawing near to our Savior to hear him, and his gracious and obliging reception of them; and obferve at the fame time, how he reprefents that fight which gave fo much offence to the pharifees, as a pleafing fpectacle to the *angels*, and the repentance of one of thofe finners as an occafion of joy in *heaven*;—and we fhall the more clearly perceive, how clofe and pertinent his apology is, and how piercing his words would be to them.

The fecond, and probably more numerous party of his audience, were the publicans and finners: and he appears to be pleading their caufe, in fome meafure, as well as his own, againft the arrogant cenfures sures of the other party. For, at the same time that he justifies his own conduct towards them, he defends also their right to be treated with candor and humanity; and, so far as they discovered a disposition to repentance, with complacency and favor. Thus far, his defence of himself, as well as his benignity of aspect and gracious deportment, had a tendency to ingratiate him in their esteem. But this was the least part of his design: mere popularity was never the object of his view: he was not disposed to indulge the prejudices, or flatter the passions, either of the scribes and pharisees, or of the publicans and sinners; and had a far nobler aim, than to gain the poor applause of this part of his audience. He meant to convert them, not to his own use, but to their own welfare and salvation. To this end, by the sheep which was gone astray, and the piece of silver which was lost, he intimates to them their unhappy and dangerous condition. By the care and diligence which were employed to recover

recover the things which were loft, he infinuates to them his own concern for them, his cordial defire of their falvation, and his readinefs to ufe his endeavors to that end. By the joy of the proprietors, when they had regained what they had loft, he fignifies the pleafure and fatisfaction it would give him, to find his endeavors effectual. And in order to add weight and dignity of fentiment to the fimplicity of the narration, he adds, that as men rejoice upon the recovery of any part of their property, fo the repentance of any one of them would not only be a pleafure to himfelf, but an occafion of joy amongft thofe benevolent fpirits above, who are mindful of and friendly to the human fpecies.

Now if we can enter thorowly into the character and fituation of thefe publicans and finners; we may be capable of feeling in fome meafure the impreffions which this reprefentation would probably make upon them. They had evidently an efteem of
our

our Savior, as a prophet of GOD, or an extraordinary teacher arifen in Ifrael; which was the motive of their affembling to hear him. They were at the fame time awed by the prefence of the pharifees and fcribes, and fenfible of the difdain with which they were looked upon by them, who were perfons refpectable for their religion and learning, and many of them for their rank and authority: they were alfo confcious of their own loofe and profligate lives. Now they would plainly underftand by our LORD's difcourfe, that though he confidered them as objects of humanity and kindnefs, and as fuch defended their caufe, as well as his own conduct, in fo admirable a manner, againft the infolence of the pharifees and fcribes: yet it was only by repentance or a change of life, that they could deferve or obtain his efteem. That being immerfed in follies and vices, they not only ftood expofed to difgrace, but were in danger of being loft for ever. But if they truly repented and became virtuous and good men,
though

though they might still be regarded with contempt and averfion by the haughty pharifees and fcribes; yet not only himfelf, but the angels of heaven would rejoice over them, and regard them with a particular pleafure and approbation. The refpect and candor, then, with which he treated them, and his defence of them againft the pharifees, muft be highly pleafing to them, and the whole reprefentation operate powerfully upon their ingenuity. They would be led to reflect upon their paft vices with a mixture of fear and fhame; and at the fame time to conceive the greateft pleafure in their own purpofes of amendment.

Thus his difcourfe was equally adapted, to convince the *pharifees and fcribes* of the rectitude of his own conduct, and to encourage the *publicans and finners* in their difpofition to repentance.

As to his own *difciples*, who formed the third party of his audience; we fhall obferve serve in another place, how they would probably be affected, both by the foregoing and following parables.

To add some general reflexions.—Benevolence or humanity is the proper temper of mind and virtue of conduct to be exercised by superiors towards their inferiors; whether that superiority consists in wealth, power, knowledge, or goodness. They who most abound in wealth should, instead of despising, most of all commiserate, and study to relieve, the wants of the poor. They who are most powerful, instead of oppressing, should think themselves peculiarly obliged to protect, the weak and defenceless. The most wise and knowing should be most willing to give information and advice to the ignorant. And the most eminent in virtue and goodness, instead of being most forward to censure and condemn, should have, nay always have, the greatest charity and candor for the vitious, and the most sincere desire of their amendment

ment and welfare. On the other hand, modesty, deference, a sensibility of their own wants or weakness, ignorance or vices, are as requisite qualities in inferiors, as benevolence and humanity in superiors. For if they show the contrary disposition; if they vainly and insolently assume a state and character which does not belong to them; they both forfeit the favor of their superiors, and render themselves incapable of receiving any real benefit from them. This is not more evidently true, or more frequently occurs, in external and worldly affairs, than in those of a moral and spiritual nature. The ignorant, if they are not sensible of their own ignorance, nor willing to be informed; if they are so conceited, as to think that they already understand every thing; not only bring upon themselves deserved scorn and contempt, but are incapable of ever becoming wise. For, *seest thou a man*, saith a truly wise author, *that is wise in his own conceit? there is more hope of a fool than of him.* So in regard

gard to the dishonest and immoral part of mankind; if they have no sense of their folly and guilt, no disposition towards repentance, but are obstinate in wickedness, and averse to moral sentiments and religious instruction; all endeavors to reclaim them are lost, or worse than lost. For to bestow instruction upon those who are thus conceited in ignorance, or hardened in wickedness is *giving that which is holy to dogs, and casting pearls before swine, who will trample them under foot, and turn again and rent you.* Our Savior himself, when he had occasion to speak before such persons, treated them with a proper and real neglect; because he spake in a manner which he knew they would not understand; and would not vouchsafe to explain himself to them, as he did to his own disciples. The publicans and sinners, who attended upon him at the time of his speaking the parables in this chapter, were of a better disposition. *They drew near to him,* saith the evangelist, *to hear him.* And from the whole of the event,

event, we may reasonably conclude, that they were in some measure of the like disposition with the publican, whom he describes as going up to the temple to pray, at the same time with a pharisee; and who *stood afar off, and would not so much as lift up his eyes to heaven, but smote upon his breast, saying, God be merciful to me a sinner.*—— If such was their disposition, they were properly qualified for our Savior's instruction, and no possible objection can remain to the propriety and humanity of his kind reception of them.

But it is no way requisite to a character of the greatest piety and humanity, that we should be forward to give advice, and to obtrude our religious and moral sentiments upon all persons indiscriminately. On the contrary, there is in this, as in all other affairs, a regard due to persons and circumstances, and a prudence in adapting means to the end; without which, though our design should be to do good, yet we may seem to discover more conceit than wisdom, and more vanity than virtue.

There are but few persons in the world, who have a right to assume extraordinary appearances of wisdom, piety, and virtue; and those few are the least forward. The scribes and pharisees assumed them in the highest degree. Our Lord, on the other hand, covered his peculiar sanctity with the most familiar behavior, his wisdom with fables and parables, and his power with the guise of poverty. But how vastly superior is that character which really is, to that which only affects to appear wise, religious, and virtuous! The latter hath indeed too often the advantage in the general opinion of the world: but the former is approved by all those superior Beings, who take cognizance of human affairs: and even among men, the most impartial and discerning will distinguish the genuine from the counterfeit.

Let

Let us endeavor to form a right judgment of human characters. Let us not be precipitate either in applauding or censuring: but at the same time preserve a due charity and candor for those whom we suppose to be the worst of mankind, and a caution of our being deceived in our opinion of those who assume to be the best.

Above all, let us examine ourselves, and try our own qualities, temper, and conduct; whether they most resemble those of the scribes and pharisees, or of the publicans and sinners, or of the true disciples of our Savior.—We are powerfully persuaded and encouraged, as his professed disciples, to aim at some resemblance even of his character, which was most eminently good and great. And assuredly, the more we imitate his example, according to our several capacities and situations, the more we shall be approved by him, and the more honor will redound to us in his everlasting kingdom.

DISCOURSE III.

Of the penitent Rake, and his compassionate Father.

LUKE XV. 11.

And he said, A certain man had two sons: and the younger of them said to his father, Father, give me the portion of goods that falleth to me. And he divided unto them his living. And not many days after, the younger son gathered all together, and took his journey into a far country, and there wasted his substance with riotous living. And when he had spent all, there arose a mighty famine in that land; and he began to be in want. And he went and joined himself to a citizen of that country; and he sent him into his fields to feed swine. And he would fain have filled his belly with the husks that the swine did eat: and no man gave unto him. And when he came to himself, he said, How many hired servants of my father's have bread enough and to spare, and I perish with hunger! I will arise, and go to my father, and will say unto him, Father, I have sinned against heaven, and before thee, and am no more worthy to be called thy son: make me as one of thy hired servants. And he arose, and came to his father. But when he was yet a great way off, his father saw him, and had compassion, and ran, and fell on his neck, and kissed him. And the son said unto him, Father, I have sinned against heaven, and in thy sight, and am no more worthy to be called thy son.—But the father said to his servants, Bring forth the best robe, and put it on him, and put a ring on his hand, and shoes on his feet: and bring hither the fatted calf, and kill it; and let us eat and be merry: for this my son was dead, and is alive again; he was lost, and is found. And they began to be merry. Now his elder son was in the field: and as he came and drew nigh to the house, he heard music and dancing. And he called one of the servants, and asked

asked what these things meant. And he said unto him, *Thy brother is come; and thy father hath killed the fatted calf, because he hath received him safe and sound. And he was angry, and would not go in: therefore came his father out, and entreated him. And he answering, said to his father, Lo, these many years do I serve thee, neither transgressed I any time thy commandment, and yet thou never gavest me a kid, that I might make merry with my friends. But as soon as this thy son was come, which hath devoured thy living with harlots, thou hast killed for him the fatted calf. And he said unto him, Son, thou art ever with me, and all that I have is thine. It was meet that we should make merry, and be glad: for this thy brother was dead, and is alive again; and was lost, and is found.*

IN pursuance of the intentions mentioned in the beginning of the last discourse, *our Savior* here proceeds to vindicate his own conduct, to confute the censures

censures of the *scribes* and *pharisees*, to expose their ill temper, to encourage the *publicans* and *sinners* in their good dispositions, and to confirm his own *disciples* in their respect and obedience, by the following pathetic and spirited narration:—In which, the repenting *prodigal* is the character designed for the *publicans and sinners*—the *father*, who receives his penitent *son* with all the marks of affection and joy, represents *our Savior* himself—and the *elder son*, who murmured at the joyful reception his *brother* met with, personates *the just men who need no repentance*; such as the murmuring *pharisees and scribes* pretended to be, tho' falsely.—We shall first give the narration itself; and then make an application of it to the several parties of *our Savior's* audience.

The parable or fable.

A certain gentleman possessed of a plentiful estate had two sons, both arrived to the age of manhood. The younger sollicited

cited his father to endow him with a fortune. The indulgent father confented, and *divided to him the portion of goods which fell to his fhare.* The youth being now mafter of his own time and fortune, confiders what fcheme of life to purfue: and foon determines to take that which appeared to his imagination the happieft. He refolved to make it his bufinefs to follow his pleafure, and to enjoy life at any expence. With this defign, he collected his fubftance together, and removed to a diftant part of the country; that being out of his father's fight or notice, and exempt from all troublefome remonftrances, he might the more freely indulge to his own inclinations. He flattered himfelf with the ample fund he was poffeffed of, and with an imagination that he could never exhauft it. Without examining, therefore, how long it would fupport him in that way of life, he very confiftently determined to give himfelf no concern about it; fuch kind of care being very difagreeable to a man of pleafure.

7.

sure. He plunges headlong into those expensive vices, which have been too fashionable amongst men of fortune in every age. But his treasure diminished apace: and before he was sufficiently aware, or would submit to the odious task of examining into the state of his affairs, all was dissipated. An unforeseen event, in the midst of his dissoluteness and extravagance, increased the consumption of his fortune, and accelerated his ruin. *A mighty famine arose in that country:* the effect of which was only reducing him the sooner to a total indigence. For he was so far from retrenching in proportion to the public scarcity, that he would not suffer his mind to be disturbed with any apprehensions of want, till downright necessity compelled him. When he had spent all, he found himself in a desperate situation, and knew not whither to betake himself for means of subsistence. His new friends, the companions of his riots and debaucheries, would contribute nothing to his support. If he had

had applied to them, it would have been to no purpose. Two other methods naturally presented themselves to his mind: either to return immediately to his father's house, and apply to him for relief; or to seek out for some employment. He preferred the latter: having quitted his father's house with gaiety and parade, he could not yet bear the thoughts of returning thither in the condition of a beggar, destitute of food and raiment. Miserable as his condition was, it had not reduced his mind in proportion to his circumstances. In this extremity, he resolved to offer his service, at any rate, and in the lowest employment, to a wealthy inhabitant of that country, who kept upon his lands a numerous herd of swine. He succeeded so far as to have his service accepted; but was sent immediately into the fields with other servants to tend the herd. Here the wretch beheld with envy the hogs devouring the husks which were before them: famine had so effectually subdued his former nicety of palate,

palate, as to create an appetite for the same food: yet no one offered him a morsel of any kind. The diftrefs now became fo oppreffive and pungent, that it awoke him as it were out of a dream: the next moment he came to himfelf: his pleafures were vanifhed, his pride humbled, and the fumes of intoxication, which blinded his underftanding, were diffipated. Sober reafon and confideration took place in his mind. He felt not only the keen fenfe of hunger, and confcious fhame of his difgraceful fervitude, but the agony of his own heart reproaching him for the folly of his paft conduct. Recollecting then that the loweft fervant in his father's houfe was in a much happier condition than himfelf; and remembering the kindnefs with which he had always been treated, he wifely refolved to rely wholly on his father's humanity and affection; and argued thus with himfelf.—" Am I, who lately lived
" in fo much affluence, now reduced to a
" condition lower than the loweft of my
" father's

"father's servants, and ready to perish for
"want? But where can I lay the blame,
"except on my own folly and extrava-
"gance? Do I not deserve to suffer? After
"having consumed my whole fortune,
"what right have I to expect support from
"a father's liberality? Have I not justly
"forfeited all the privileges of my birth
"and family? I cannot expect to be re-
"ceived in the quality of a son: I cannot
"have the confidence to desire it. If I can
"be admitted into his house in the capa-
"city of a menial servant, and earn my
"bread by labor, it's all the favor I ought
"to expect, and all I will request. I will
"immediately return to my father, and
"acknowledge to him in the fullest terms,
"how much I have abused, how entirely I
"have forfeited, the bounty of heaven and
"the kindness of a father; and make it
"my earnest request to be admitted into
"his house as an hired servant." With
these resolutions he set forward towards
his father's house.

The father might not want information of his son's conduct or condition, during the time of his absence. But having made him independent, he had left him wholly to his own disposal; and hearing of his extravagances, his mind would forebode nothing but the most disgraceful and miserable conclusion. He looked upon him as in the worst of dangers, born down by the torrent of his lust towards the gulph of destruction, nay, as already *dead* and *lost for ever*. During the course of his voluptuousness he kept a painful silence: and when he heard afterward of the indigence and misery he was reduced to in consequence of it, suppressed the tenderness of his disposition, and resolved to take no step towards his relief, but at all events to wait for his return, before he would shew him any favor. But as soon as he was apprised, that his misery had brought him to the use of his reason and a sense of his folly, and that he was upon his return, with an intent to make confession, and implore relief;

lief; then, with the consent of his judgment, he gave a loose to his affection; and when his son was yet at a considerable distance, *saw him, and had compassion*; and, notwithstanding the meanness of his present appearance, and the unworthiness of his past conduct, hastened to embrace him. He did not doubt of the sincerity of his repentance, because he knew him to be of an ingenuous temper, and believed that nothing but an ungovernable thirst of pleasure had prevailed over his judgment and better dispositions, and transported him to such a desperate extravagance; and therefore received him with *this* mark of paternal affection, even before he had uttered a word. The youth finding himself received with such a cordial tenderness and generosity, instead of the resentments and reproaches he was conscious of deserving, began with great earnestness to repeat the acknowledgments which he intended to make, declared himself unworthy of the *name* of a son to such a father; and was going to urge his requeft, to be admitted on the terms of *a hired fervant,* when the father's affection interpofed: he conceived the purport of what he was going to fay, and generoufly interrupts him, by giving orders to the fervants to entertain him immediately in the moft liberal and elegant manner; adding with a tranfport of joy, *For this my fon was dead, but is alive again; and was loft, but is found.*

The elder brother was affected in a very different manner. Returning from the fields where he had been employed about the paternal eftate, when he came near to the houfe, ignorant of what had paffed, and perceived fuch unufual marks of joy as mufic and dancing, he was furprized: and calling out one of the fervants he inquired of him what they meant? and was informed by him, the occafion was, the fafe arrival of his brother. Hearing this imperfect account, he was feized with a fpirit of envy and jealoufy—he looked upon it as as a flagrant inſtance of partiality in his father to his younger ſon, who had acted ſo unworthily—conſidered himſelf as neglected and affronted, and was fired with reſentment and diſdain—accordingly, he refuſed to go in and ſee his brother. Information of this being brought to the father, he was immediately apprehenſive, that the tranſaction might appear, through miſtake, in a diſagreeable light to his elder ſon; and therefore came out and entreated him. In conſequence of which, the ſon laid open the ſuppoſed grievance, and expreſſed his diſcontent and indignation in the following manner: "Have I not juſt "cauſe of reſentment? Have I not ſerved "you theſe many years, like a faithful and "diligent ſteward of your eſtate? and "always been obſervant of your com-"mands? And is this the favor and reward "I meet with for my conſtant duty? When "was I permitted to entertain my friends "with ſuch marks of liberality and ſplen-"dor? But as ſoon as this ſon of yours "was

"was come, who has confumed all the
"fortune you fo lately gave him, and
"whofe infamous conduct has been the
"difgrace of the family; he is entertained
"with a joy and pleafure equal to his ex-
"travagance. All favor, affection, and
"liberality are referved for him."

THE father heard his complaints with the greateft calmnefs and attention: and apprehending that there was fomething more in his mind than he had expreffed, and that his jealoufy was fo ftrong as to lead him to fufpect, that the fortune which his brother had expended was to be fupplyed out of the paternal eftate,—affured him "that all his fufpicions were ground-
"lefs—that he well remembered his duti-
"ful behavior—that he would always
"give him the preference in his efteem,
"and never difappoint his juft expecta-
"tions—that the rejoicing which he made
"at that time, was not owing to any par-
"tial affection, but to an extraordinary
"and

" and moſt happy occaſion, *viz*. the re-
" covery of a ſon, whom he had before
" deſpaired of as loſt irrecoverably:"—
and intimated, " how unnatural it was,
" that the ſame event, which was the juſt
" cauſe of ſo much joy to a father, ſhould
" give ſo much diſcontent to a brother."
Son, ſaid he, you are ever with me, and all that I have is yours. But it is meet that we ſhould rejoice (you as well as myſelf) *on this happy occaſion: for this your brother was dead, and is alive again; was loſt, and is found.*

Now to make an application of the foregoing parable to our Savior's audience.— Here was a great cauſe depending between two conſiderable parties, the *ſcribes and phariſees*, and the *publicans and ſinners*; and his diſciples, who formed a third party, ſate as judges of the whole procedure. He immediately compoſes and relates to them this fable, without any apparent premeditation. What effect it had upon the audience we are not expresly informed. But it is easy to perceive, how pertinent it was to the occasion; and natural to infer from it, the benignity of our Savior's disposition, the serenity of his temper, his presence of mind, exactness of judgment, and facility of invention. What stronger instance could he give of his own invincible goodness of temper and divine genius, than to compose a narration so full of natural, pleasing, and pathetic images, in contrast to the ill temper, and in answer to the provoking language of an opponent party?

THE two aforementioned parties were *brother-Jews* to each other, like the *two sons* in the parable, and as widely different in their temper and character. All persons addicted to sensual vices were branded among the Jews with the appellation of sinners. The publicans also, by their very office of levying the taxes in the service of the Roman government, were very odious among their countrymen. Though that office

office was not unlawful in itself, or inconsistent with a character of integrity and virtue; yet the religious casuists amongst the Jews determined otherwise. It was a controverted point amongst them, whether it was lawful to *pay* tribute to *Cæsar*. This question they put to our Savior, hoping to reduce him to a dilemma, and gain an advantage against him. As they disputed, then, the lawfulness of *paying* tribute; so we may be certain, they all agreed in pronouncing it unlawful to *collect* it. Those Jews, therefore, who accepted that office, immediately lost all reputation, and became so infamous, that the name of a *publican* was thought to imply the worst qualities that can disgrace human nature. It may be justly supposed then, that the publicans were in general men of dissolute morals: for it is not probable, that a Jew of any rank, fortune, or *character* would make interest for such an office, or accept it, unless, like the *prodigal son*, he had reduced himself to a necessity of entering into such a disgraceful service for a support:

port: a service as base, in the opinion of the Jews, as *tending a herd of swine*, animals of which they had the greatest abhorrence. Yet it is probable, that some of these publicans present were the *younger* branches of considerable families, who had reduced themselves to this necessity by their extravagances. And in regard to others of them, their vices might be the consequence, though not the cause of their engaging in that office. For virtue is sometimes practised more for the sake of the reputation attending it, than from any other motive: and many persons, when they have once lost their honor, seem to think their virtue hardly worth preserving; and hence become desperate and abandoned in their conduct.—The vices of the pharisees and scribes, were chiefly covetousness, pride, and hypocrisy: those of the publicans and sinners, intemperance, incontinence, and prodigality. But the latter were notwithstanding of a far better disposition than the former, and more capable

pable of reformation. They were conscious of their own follies and vices, and had some compunction of mind for them; at least, they did not *justify themselves;* and pretend, like the pharisees, to be holy and religious men. They attended upon our Savior at this time on purpose to hear him, with a high veneration of him, and with marks of humility and repentance. He, like the good *father* in the parable, received them as penitents, with a singular tenderness and compassion, entertained them with agreeable marks of affection and kindness; and knowing their sensibility of mind and ingenuity of temper, which rendered them capable of being wrought upon, was willing to give them the strongest possible encouragement to repentance. To this end he applyed the most engaging behavior, pertinent instructions, and striking representations. With what surprize would they see *themselves* personated in the character and conduct of the *prodigal son?* they found themselves

at

at unawares fitting before our Savior for their picture, which he drew for them inftantly, and as it were with one ftroke of his pencil. We may fairly prefume, that they had fenfe enough to know their own *likenefs*; and would clearly underftand, thofe of them efpecially, who had confumed their fortunes by their extravagances, whom the diffolute and penitent youth was defigned to reprefent; and therefore would mark the feveral incidents befalling him, and liften to the conclufion of the ftory with the utmoft attention. Nothing can be conceived more admirably adapted to their character and fituation. When we confider the prodigal fon as their *reprefentative*, and obferve the deplorable fituation to which he had reduced himfelf—the unfeigned repentance he difcovered—his intended requeft to be admitted into his father's houfe, not as a fon, of which he declared himfelf unworthy, but as a hired fervant—and on the other hand, the readinefs of the father in going out to meet him—the compaffion and tendernefs with which he embraced him—the cordial welcome with which he received him, not as a hired fervant, but as a fon—the joyful entertainment which he made on that occafion—and the anfwer he gives to the angry remonftrance of the elder fon;—the whole defcription is fo beautifully expreffive of the fentiments of ingenuous repentance proper to the publicans and finners, and of the paternal goodnefs, prudence, and affection of our Savior, correfponding to fuch fentiments in them, that it could not fail of making an irrefiftible impreffion upon the hearts of *this part* of his audience.

BUT his obliging behavior to the publicans and finners gave the higheft offence to the other party, the pharifees and fcribes. Like the *elder fon*, they were fired with refentment and difdain: they would not vouchfafe to go in and fit down to meat with fuch company; whom they looked

looked upon (though brother-Jews) with the utmoſt contempt and averſion. They not only put the worſt conſtruction upon our Savior's conduct, but reſented it, as a perſonal ſlight and indignity offered to them, and an inſtance of ſcandalous partiality, in appearing to pay more attention and reſpect to ſuch vile perſons than to themſelves: and, in conſequence, not only murmured amongſt themſelves, but proceeded to inſult and reproach him for it. He anſwers them by the parables contained in this chapter. And we may obſerve, that when he had carried on the narration of the father and his two ſons, to the point in which it moſt exactly correſponded to the diſpoſition himſelf and the two parties of his audience were in, at the very moment he was ſpeaking to them; he there cloſes it, and leaves them to gueſs what effect the father's obliging and pathetic anſwer had upon the mind of *the elder ſon*, who was the *repreſentative* of the *phariſees and ſcribes*, or rather of what they pretended

tended to be, *the juſt men who need no repentance.*

It is evident, that he vindicates his own conduct even upon their own ſuppoſition, that they were really, in compariſon of the other party, righteous and good men, conſtant obſervers of the laws of God, like the elder ſon, who had never tranſgreſſed his father's commands.—The only objection which they could make to his conduct with any colour of reaſon, was this: that he ſeemed to make no diſtinction between perſons of the greateſt virtue and the worſt of profligates, provided they came to him with marks of repentance; but treated them with equal reſpect, or rather gave the preference to the latter. This objection he removes in the concluſion of the parable, by the father's anſwer to the elder ſon's remonſtrance: *Son, you are ever with me, and all that I have is yours.* Whatever affection, then, he diſcovered for his younger ſon, he did not mean to advance him

him who had been guilty of such misconduct to an equal degree of favor and esteem, or to deprive the elder of any preference due to him on account of his constant service and obedience. *All that I have,* says he, *is yours: but it is meet that we should rejoice and be glad. For this your brother was dead, but is alive again; and was lost, but is found.* So notwithstanding the condescension and kindness which our Savior discovered to the penitent publicans and sinners; he did not mean to detract from the superior worth of such as had never been guilty of the like vicious practices. On the contrary, he gave them the preference in his esteem: but at the same time, it was perfectly natural, humane, and worthy of the best character, to conceive a particular satisfaction and joy in the reformation of offenders.

The propriety and beauty with which he describes his own disposition and character, in that of the father in the parable,

ble, highly deserves our attention and admiration. Some of these scribes and pharisees were distinguished by the appellation of masters and *fathers:* but whether they or he had more of the true *paternal* disposition, they might easily understand from this representation. Yet we have ground to suspect that they were not in the least convinced or satisfied, even with an apology so singular, so pertinent, and affecting. No representations can be satisfactory to those who are previously determined to resist conviction : no strength of argument, propriety of adress, or excellence of discourse, will make an impression upon minds hardened by inveterate prejudice.

The main sentiment in these parables is this :—that the recovery of any human creature, from vice and misery, to virtue and happiness, is an event pleasing to every good mind.—A sentiment to which the scribes and pharisees appear to have been strangers. They were utterly destitute of that

that candor and benevolence to the low and diffolute part of the human fpecies, which is a principle characteriftic of a noble mind. Addicted to their own intereft, they were regardlefs of the welfare of others: elevated to rank and diftinction, they were infolent to their inferiors: affuming the character of religious perfons, they were cenforious upon the vices of their neighbors: wrapt up in their own importance, and governed by felfifh affections, they had no conception of that moft generous concern for and delight in the reformation and happinefs of mankind, which was our Savior's diftinguifhed character; and by which he *merited* the glorious title of *the Son of GOD.*

HITHERTO we may obferve, he contents himfelf with vindicating his own difpofition and conduct againft their cenfures, without any apparent and direct recrimination. But we fhall find in the fequel, that he perfectly knew what fort of men he he had to contend with; and accordingly begins to attack their vices, and to expofe their hypocrify and villany, by exhibiting the character of *the unjuſt ſteward*. But before we proceed to that, we ſhall make, in the following difcourfe, fome general reflections on the preceding parable.

DISCOURSE IV.

Of the penitent Rake, and his compassionate Father.

LUKE XV. 11.

And he said, A certain man had two sons, &c.

I Have ventured, in the preceding discourse, to exhibit this parable in a diffuse and modern style; though sensible how far I have hereby deviated from its original concisenefs and divine simplicity, and enervated the force and spirit of it. For the quick succession of incidents, the sudden transitions, the surprizing as well as pathetic strokes of dialogue, would make it to penetrate with a more pointed force, like lightning, into the hearts of his audience. But a paraphrastic narration may be useful to us, for the sake of explanation, and in order to make the application

plication of it to the general circumstances of mankind more easy.

We shall proceed to consider it as an exact picture of human nature, and the several characters as drawn from real life: shall endeavor to shew the propriety of its several parts: and add such reflections as they naturally lead to.

The first thing observable in the conduct of the dissolute youth, is his solliciting his father to endow him with a fortune.—— To be free, independent, masters of their own time, and of a plentiful estate, is a situation all young persons naturally aspire to, without knowing the dangers attending it. Through want of judgment and experience, they are easily imposed upon, and forward to deceive themselves. They have no distrust of those gay ideas which flutter in their brain; and are confident, that the world, and the enjoyment of it, are no other than such as their warm imaginations

ginations paint them. Whereas, liberty, wealth, and power, in the hands of those who know not how to use them, are like *edge-tools*, with which the unskilful handler *maims* or wounds himself.

The youth had no sooner received his fortune, than blindly following his inclinations to luxury and pleasure, he dissipated in a short time the whole of it.——— This may appear to some an improbable circumstance; and that he could not be so utterly destitute of recollection and forethought, as to consume without reserve, and to the last mite. But, beside the additional circumstance of a famine, to render it more probable, this part of the description is too often verified in human life. There are too many examples in modern times, that prove, to what degrees of extravagance and dissipation, the indulged love of grandeur and pleasure will hurry men. Are there not some in this age and nation, who are now indulging to luxury and excefs, though they know, that they have already confumed all their own fortune, and are fquandering away the property of other men? how often do perfons act as if they had not the leaft confideration, of what their own condition of life will certainly be, in a very fhort compafs of time?—the youth in the parable only acted *confiftently* in proceeding as he had begun. For the fame reafon, and in the fame manner, that he fet out in the purfuit of pleafure, he continued in it as long as was poffible. It is eafy to indulge to pleafure and expence: *wide is the gate and broad is the way.* But to draw back, to retrench, to break off vicious habits, and bid adieu to beloved pomp and pleafure, requires much wifdom and ftrength of refolution. Indeed, they who have no concern about their own condition in another life, and to eternity, are very *confiftent*, in throwing off at the fame time all care about their future fubfiftence in this world.

world. For if the hope of salvation and fear of damnation be not sufficient to restrain men from vicious pursuits, why should any other motive prevail? If religion have no effect, why should worldly prudence have any? To be reduced to beggary and disgrace in this world, is indeed a terrible consequence; but certainly not equal to that of being condemned by the judgment of GOD, and exposed to eternal ruin. If the dread of this makes no impression, why should the fear of any thing else be effectual? If voluptuousness be indeed your supreme good, and you can sacrifice to it, virtue, honor, and the hope of immortality, why not every thing else? If another world be not worthy of consideration, there is little reason to disturb our minds about consequences in this. Pursue pleasure at all adventures, regardless of whatever may follow in any part of futurity: for this is only acting up to the perfection of the character.

As soon as the prodigal youth found himself reduced to indigence, and in the midst of famine, it might be supposed, that the first and most obvious method he would think of for a support, would be returning to his father's house, and that he would immediately resolve upon it. But this procedure would not have been so true a copy of human nature. They who have been guilty of great vices and extravagances, though convinced in their own minds, yet are seldom brought to make a full acknowledgement, without down-right necessity: it appears to them as the lowest submission and most grievous mortification: to avoid which, they will put matters to any hazard, and endure almost any misery. They conceive a certain false shame, pride, and obstinacy, which is connected and confounded, in their imaginations, with a sense of honor and greatness of mind, though in fact very remote from it. There is a magnanimity and ingenuity of spirit in frankly confessing an error: but persisting

persisting in it, is the effect of something very different. It is universally allowed, that all men are subject to errors and faults: why then should they feel so much reluctance in acknowledging them? there is wisdom in retracting our mistakes, and dignity in repenting of our faults. Infallibility is indeed the highest wisdom; but infinitely above human nature. The highest we can possibly attain to, is an habitual readiness to receive information and conviction, that we may be continually growing wiser.

However, in the instance before us, another difficulty would naturally occur to the mind of this unhappy youth. For after being guilty of such unbounded excess, not all his experience of his father's affection could make him certain, what kind of reception he should meet with, and free him from all doubt and fear about the issue. And should his father prove inexorable, as well as his brother imbittered against

against him; should he find himself abandoned by them to the consequences of his own folly, notwithstanding any confession or intreaty he might make; this would appear more terrible and insupportable than any present slavery he could endure. It was proper, therefore, to represent him as preferring the meanest employment by which he could hope to earn bread; and his distress, as aggravated even to the last extremity, before he is described as coming to himself, and taking up the wise resolution of applying to his father for relief. Accordingly, hunger, shame, and slavery are all added, as requisite to give an edge to his reflections, to conquer his disdain, and thorowly subdue his mind to his circumstances.

But the aforesaid resolution being once fixed in his mind, by the operation of so cogent motives, and his attention rightly directed; things began to appear to him in a very different light: the happy effect of of which may be obferved, in the ingenuous acknowledgments and modeft requeft which he refolved to make; and which admirably comport with his character and fituation. He confeffes, before a queftion was afked, without the leaft difguife or palliation, and in the fulleft terms, his guilt and unworthinefs: and all he defired, was only to be admitted in the capacity of an hired fervant, that he might earn the neceffaries of life by labor; and this, not as a matter of right, but of favor and indulgence.—Here is an exquifite propriety in the reprefentation. He could not poffibly ufe expreffions more fuitable to his condition, or give a ftronger proof of the fenfibility of his mind, and the fincerity of his repentance. Had he approached his father with an air of fturdy confidence; and prefuming upon his birth, made a bold demand of being reftored to his former ftate of honor and plenty, or of a fupply proportioned to the fortune he had confumed; this would have been giving, not

marks

marks of repentance, but of an unconquerable infolence and profligacy of mind. Or if he had endeavored to palliate his conduct by artful excufes, and to impofe upon his father by a falfe account; this would have implied fuch a difingenuity, as would have left little room to hope for an amendment.

Let us now contemplate the beautiful image of paternal prudence and affection next exhibited.—The firft thing obfervable is his indulgence in yielding to his fon's requeft. Here it may be objected, that as he muft probably have difcovered before this fome fymptoms of his fon's propenfity to voluptuoufnefs; why did he yield, and hereby impower him to purfue his inclination? It is a diminution of his character, to fuppofe that he was prevailed upon by mere dint of importunity, to do an act which appeared to be of dangerous confequence.——Let us confider, whether other motives might not have been equally or more prevalent. Might not a refusal be attended with as bad consequences as a compliance? might it not be imputed (whether justly or not) to a spirit of tyranny or avarice, or a groundless distrust? might it not alienate his son's affection, create disgust and aversion, or tempt him to some violent course?—when young persons are arrived at manhood, to find themselves still kept wholly in dependence, and treated as in a state of minority, appears to them (especially in some circumstances) very unreasonable. On the other hand, by consenting, he gave an eminent proof of affection to his son, of a confidence in him, and a reliance on the professions which he may be supposed to make, of sobriety, and a prudent use of the wealth he should become possessed of: professions, which might be sincere in some measure; as he had not yet learned, by dearly purchased experience, the strength of his own passions, and the weakness of his resolution. There is then sufficient ground to suppose,

suppose, that the father might act in this instance with deliberation and prudence. Nothing in the parental office requires more judgment, than to know, in many cases, what to grant or to refuse. It is sometimes difficult to forsee the consequences of either; sometimes easy to foresee great inconveniences from both. In such a situation, all that can be done is to compare the probable consequences on each side, in order to avoid the greater evil or danger. Restraint may be equally useful or hurtful as indulgence: and much penetration is sometimes requisite to determine which is preferable, or to find out and observe a just medium.

One part of the son's intention, in taking up his residence in a distant part of the country, might be, that his father should not be acquainted with his manner of life. But a parent's intelligence often reaches further than youths apprehend: the world is for the most part ready enough to to give intelligence of any perſons miſconduct or misfortune; and often to exaggerate them by falſe reports. Yet there is not the leaſt intimation of the father's uſing any means in order to reclaim his ſon, or of any correſpondence between them. Silence is often more ſignificant than language: and where it is neceſſary to uſe words of reproof, the fewer the better. To pour out a torrent of reproaches is often more provoking than convincing: and to repeat admonitions and advices, is diminiſhing the weight in proportion to the quantity; and wearying the patience, rather than winning the affection of the perſon adviſed. One expreſſion well-timed and directed, like an arrow that goes ſtraight to the mark, will have more effect than a multitude of random advices, which are only ſhot into the air. When perſons are arrived at maturity; if their own judgment and conſideration will not ſerve to direct them aright, it is but ſeldom that good counſel will answer the purpose. When parental authority naturally ceases, it is in vain to assume it: friendly persuasion alone is to be used in the stead of it: and it requires much discretion to administer it in a proper and effectual manner.

Though the father might be well-informed of the destitute condition to which the son had reduced himself; yet he was not influenced by a weak compassion to send him any supply; but wisely left him to take his own course, and to suffer the consequence of his folly; till by bitter experience and reflexion he should come to himself, and of his own accord, from the conviction of his own mind, resolve to acknowledge his misconduct, and seek a reconciliation. From this example of paternal prudence and resolution, we may take occasion to observe two errors in the conduct of parents, opposite to each other, and equally to be avoided; one proceeding from a too gentle and affectionate, the other from

from a too rigid and implacable temper. The offending party always ought to make the first advances: and in every instance similar to that which is represented in the parable, it is absolutely necessary. If parents pass over gross instances of misconduct in their children, without any marks of displeasure; or if after expressing a resentment, they are too speedily or easily appeased; if they are the first to seek for reconciliation, as if themselves were the criminal party, it tends to encourage the licentiousness of youth, and embolden them in vicious practices. It should be thought an indispensable condition, that the offender should first acknowledge his error: But on the other hand, as soon as ingenuous acknowledgments are made, with proofs of a real intention of amendment, then to continue obdurate and inflexible, and maintain a spirit of resentment or disdain, is still more unwise and pernicious: for instead of encouraging their good purposes, it tends to break the natural honefty and ingenuity of their minds, and drive them into defperate courfes. Befide, where may forgivenefs be hoped for; where are lenity and compaffion to be found, if not in the heart of a parent? An implacable irreconcileable fpirit is contrary to humanity in any perfon; but in a parent moft unnatural. When the licentious and diffolute youth was changed into the fober penitent, and modeft fuppliant, when the father faw him approaching in fuch circumftances of diftrefs, with lively anguifh and remorfe apparent in his countenance, he was melted with compaffion; and when he heard his candid confeffion, was not only reconciled, but tranfported with joy: and fuch was his generofity of mind and ftrength of affection, that he would not give his fon the pain of uttering, or himfelf of hearing, the humble requeft to be admitted as a fervant; but immediately, with a kind view to diffipate the fear and dejection of his fon's mind, ordered a feaft to be prepared, accompanied with

with all the usual demonstrations of cheerfulness and pleasure, upon account of his happy return.——If then there was the least spark of ingenuity in the son's breast, he could not but be strongly affected on this occasion; when instead of the contempt and reproaches which he was conscious of deserving, he found himself received with such a cordial respect and pleasure, as he could hardly imagine to himself: when he found even the greatness of his distress equalled by the tenderness of his reception, and the sincerity of his repentance exceeded by his father's goodness.

The elder son appears to have been of a sober frugal industrious temper, intent upon improving the paternal estate, and withal austere and rigid, mindful of his own interest, not very susceptible of the tender and humane affections, and of less ingenuity and sensibility of heart than the younger: and therefore, a jealousy, lest his brother's return fhould interfere with his intereft and filial rights, was uppermoft in his mind: which, together with a fufpicion of his father's partiality, tempted him to break out in a fudden angry remonftrance; without difcovering any compaffion for his brother, or fatisfaction at his fafe arrival. The father ftudies not only to calm his refentments, and to remove his fufpicion, but to enkindle an affection in his mind towards his brother.

Now from this temper of the elder fon, and the father's behavior to him, we may obferve, that it is a part of parental prudence, to avoid carefully all appearances of partiality; efpecially in favor of fuch of their children as have rendered themfelves lefs worthy of their affection.—And whenever fuch appearances occur accidentally, or cannot properly be avoided, then to be ready to explain them, in order to remove, as foon as may be, the jealoufy and

and diftruft which they may occafion—to encourage alfo fuch as think themfelves aggrieved, to lay open their complaints with all decent freedom, in order to their receiving all fuch information and fatiffaction as circumftances will admit—And finally to condefcend fo far, as to acknowledge an error, if they have committed one in matters of any confequence: which may be done, fo as not to diminifh, but rather increafe, filial refpect and confidence.—But all this is to be practifed in proportion to their children's age, and capacity of forming a right judgment.

It is equally incumbent upon young perfons, efpecially during their minority, to beware of conceiving a difguft againft their parents—to be always willing to put an entire confidence in them—to fuppofe that they have reafons for their conduct, even where there is room for fufpicion—and to efteem it a mark of favor, if they vouchfafe to explain thofe reafons; and a proof of goodnefs, if ever they acknowledge a miftake.

We fhall conclude with obferving, in a general and fummary view, the ftructure and moral application of this excellent parable.

As to the ftructure of it—the contraft between the diffolute youth's *feafting luxurioufly with harlots*, and defiring to *fill his belly with the food of the hogs*; his removal from his father, in order to indulge himfelf in *riot and excefs*, and his return to him, in order to obtain *neceffaries*; the neglect which he experienced in his diftrefs from the *world*, and the generous reception he met with from a *father*:—the proportion and correfpondence of the father's *compaffion* to the fon's *diftrefs*, *satiffaction* to his *acknowledgments*, and *joy* to his happy *recovery*:—the delicacy of *preventing* his humble requeft to be admitted as a fervant:—the difdain of the elder fon in refusing to see the younger, or give him the title of brother, and stiling him *this son of yours*;—the father's soft insinuation to him, in saying *it was meet that WE should rejoice*, and changing his former expression, *this MY SON*, into, *this YOUR BROTHER:*——these are strokes so perfectly natural, and have such an easy propriety and elegance, that they cannot fail of giving great pleasure, as well as instruction, to a judicious reader.

In a moral application of the whole to human life—we may observe the miserable condition to which vice often, and sometimes speedily, reduces men;—to poverty, disease, infamy, or death: particularly the vices of intemperance, lewdness, and luxury, to which youth is most inclined.—As soon as young persons are left at full liberty, they are most liable to reduce themselves to slavery—when wealth is suddenly poured upon them, they are in danger of poverty—the more they study to gratify their

their inclinations, the more difappointment and mortification they will meet with— the more eagerly they purfue pleafure, the more certainly the excurfion will terminate in a region of pain and forrow. But even when immerfed in follies and vices, they are ftill objects of pity and humanity. And if ever they have the wifdom and grace to repent fincerely and acknowledge their errors; their acknowledgments fhould be accepted with a particular fatisfaction and joy, themfelves be reftored to favor, and their miftakes blotted out of the book of every man's remembrance.

DISCOURSE V.

Of the subtle Steward, or hardened Villain.

LUKE xvi. 1, &c. to 8.

And he said also unto his disciples, There was a certain rich man which had a steward; and the same was accused unto him that he had wasted his goods. And he called him, and said unto him, How is it that I hear this of thee? give an account of thy stewardship; for thou mayest be no longer steward. Then the steward said within himself, What shall I do? for my lord taketh away from me the stewardship: I cannot dig; to beg I am ashamed.——I am resolved what to do; that when I am put out of the stewardship, they may receive me into their houses. So he called every one of his lord's debtors unto him; and said unto the first, How much owest thou unto my lord? And he said, An hundred measures of oil. And he said unto him,

him, Take thy bill, and fit down quickly, and write fifty. Then faid he to another, And how much oweft thou? And he faid, An hundred meafures of wheat. And he faid unto him, Take thy bill, and write fourfcore. And the lord commended the unjuft fteward, becaufe he had done wifely.

THOUGH it cannot be made to appear with certainty, that this parable was fpoke immediately after thofe of the foregoing chapter, and to the fame audience; yet it feems very probable, from the manner in which the evangelift introduces it, *(And he faid alfo to his difciples)* and from the mention which is afterwards made of the pharifees being prefent, and giving attention to what was faid, v. 14. *The pharifees alfo, who were covetous, heard all thefe things.* In fpeaking the former, our Savior directed his countenance and voice to the fcribes and pharifees; but in this, to his own difciples, who formed a diftinct part from the reft of his audience. And

And his main intention appears to have been, to extirpate from their minds that selfish fraudulent and designing temper, which he perceived in the pharisees and scribes, and which is the character in general of the men of this world.

We shall first give the narration itself. Secondly, remark in general the propriety and consistency of it. Thirdly, consider the application, which our Savior himself makes of it, to his own disciples. And fourthly, how far the scribes and pharisees were affected by it.

First, the narration or fable.

There was a certain gentleman, who kept a steward, whom he confided in so intirely as to impower him to manage all his estates, receive his rents and profits, and give discharges. If the steward then had had a proper sense of honor and gratitude; this confidence would have been a strong tye to fidelity, and have led

led him to conceive the greatest abhorrence of betraying so absolute a trust, and injuring so generous a master. But with him it had the contrary effect. For to a dishonest mind, opportunity itself is a prevailing temptation, and the greater the trust is, he will the more certainly abuse it. So the steward considered the confidence his master put in him in no other light, than as the effect of his weak credulity, and a fortunate opportunity for himself to serve his own ends. He resolved to gratify his pride and pleasure at his master's expence; and flattered himself, that he had blinded him so effectually, and could manage affairs so artfully, as to escape all discovery: at least, he trusted to his own cunning to bring himself off with impunity. He went on therefore without scruple or remorse, committing all the frauds that he thought consistent with his own safety, proceeding from smaller to greater, till he became very expert in artifice, and thorowly hardened in villany.

His lord was not apt to harbor fuspicions of his fervants, nor willing to think, that one, in whom he had repofed fo great a confidence, could be guilty of fo much bafenefs and treachery. But by degrees his eyes were opened: accufations were multiplied and fupported by fuch undeniable teftimony, that he was at length fenfible how much he had been abufed, and thorowly convinced of his fervant's villany. He then fummoned him into his prefence: and after expreffing with a ftern countenance his aftonifhment and indignation, ordered him to make up his accompts inftantly: for he was refolved to difcharge him from the ftewardfhip, as foon as they were fettled.

The fteward upon this was thrown into a terrible confternation. He was fully aware, that all was difcovered; and was too confcious of what he had done to conceive any hope of juftifying himfelf, or of regaining his mafter's favor. But inftead

of reflecting upon his own treachery, or conceiving any design of making reparation to his master, or of changing his own conduct; his whole concern was, that he could no longer live splendidly, as he had done, upon his master's fortunes; but must lose his place, and be reduced to difficulties for a maintenance. As soon as he was alone, such thoughts as these crouded into his mind,—" That as he was going to lose his
" place, and consequently his livelihood,
" he must immediately invent some other
" method of support—that considering how
" well he had lived in the world, it would
" be impossible for him now to earn his
" bread by the sweat of his brows—and as
" to the mean trade of begging, he could
" not bear the thoughts of submitting to
" that--nor indeed could he expect much fa-
" vour from the world, if his master's reports
" against him were credited——all would
" be rather disposed to shut their doors
" against him; and so he would be reduced
" to starve, or take the last remedy despair
" would

"would suggest. It was necessary to think
"of something to save appearances, pre-
"serve his reputation, and gain friends."—
Here he makes a pause, sets his invention to
work, and presently comes out with his
device. He recollected that the power was
yet in his hands, and resolved to make use
of it. He found an advantage from his
lord's imprudence, in not discharging him
immediately, and sending notice to his
tenants and debtors to keep no further accompts with him. For tho' he could not
amass any thing directly to himself, yet he
could remit as much as he pleased to them,
and thereby lay such an obligation upon
them, that they would not suffer him to
starve; especially, as he intended to persuade them, that his master had used him
ill, and deprived him of his office and support, purely upon the account of his good
nature and generosity.

Having laid his scheme then, and being
sensible he had no time to lose, he immediately

diately applies to all his lord's tenants and debtors, and makes an enquiry into the refpective fums which were due from them. And the better to conceal the defign againft his mafter, and the iniquity of his procedure, he would not remit the whole of what they owed; but pretended to take their feveral cafes into confideration; and expreffed a defire of compounding their feveral debts in an equitable and generous manner: affuring them, " That it had al-
" ways been his main purpofe and ambi-
" tion to do that which was juft and fair
" between his mafter and them:"—throwing out many hints, " That though his
" mafter was very wealthy, and could well
" afford to make abatements, and would,
" if he had but common humanity; yet it
" muft be owned, that he was too near
" himfelf, and too ready to fqueeze and
" opprefs his poor tenants and fervants,—
" but that for his own part, he always
" confidered how hard times and tenures
" were—that *his confcience* would not fuf-
" fer

"fer him to take from them as much as
"might be strictly due by law, and that
"he thought himself bound to stand by
"the reason and equity of the case, and to
"do to them as he would be done to him-
"self."—So he gave a discharge to each for as much as he thought proper, and entered the remainder in the books of accompt. No doubt then, but they all went away highly satisfied, and well prepared to throw the blame of his dismission upon his master, to think that he had been unjustly suspected and hardly treated, and to conclude themselves obliged in gratitude to shew him all the friendship in their power, because he had been so good a man, and so much their friend.

The lord never imagined that his steward could contrive, in so short a time, and after the notice he had given him, to commit any more frauds. When he came to be informed therefore how he had been employed, and in what manner he had
made

made up his accompts; though he could not but conceive a high resentment of such procedure, yet at the same time he could not forbear expressing a surprize at finding himself so egregiously outwitted, and an admiration of the man's contrivance. For in one minute of recollection he had hit upon the only expedient, by which he could extricate himself from his present difficulties, and save himself from utter disgrace and ruin; nay, even gain friends at his master's expence, and reputation by his own dishonesty: Insomuch, that notwithstanding all the villanies his master could justly charge him with, he would find most people ready to befriend him, to vindicate his character, and to impute his dismission to a suspiciousness and severity of temper in his lord, and not to any want of honesty in him. So much sagacity and address appeared in this, that the lord confessed, "That he was the wisest man to "serve his own ends that he had ever met "with; and had taken the most prudent "and

"and consistent measures for his own sup-
"port, that his temper and situation would
"admit."

HAVING thus drawn at full length the character designed by our Savior, we shall add some remarks upon it. And in the first place, we may compare it to that of the prodigal son in the foregoing parable. He was the man of *pleasure only*; and acted consistently, in pursuing it to the utmost, and to his own ruin. But it does not appear that he wanted honesty: for though he wasted his substance in riotous living, yet it was *his own:* and when reduced to extremity, he rather chose to enter into the meanest service, by which he could earn bread, than take any dishonest methods for a support. On the other hand, the steward was the man of *business also*, and wasted *his master*'s substance: and was not scrupulous in the least of repeating his frauds even after a detection; but prudently resolved to finish in the same style as he had begun. He appears then, upon a juſt compariſon, to be of a worſe character, and more incorrigible, than the other. Hence, our Savior, with perfect judgment and propriety, repreſents the former as brought to repentance; but the latter, as hardened in wickedneſs.—It is worth obſerving, how the ſteward pleads *neceſſity* in excuſe of his intended villany: a neceſſity founded merely on his own indolence or pride. *I cannot dig: to beg I am aſhamed.* Such are the excuſes men often make to themſelves for their diſhoneſty: and it is the temper of too many in the world, to be more afraid of poverty than of villany; and to excuſe to themſelves their own frauds, by putting upon them the color of neceſſity.

2. We may obſerve the perfect conſiſtency of the character here exhibited. The ſame manner of thinking and acting is preſerved throughout. The ſteward never once thought of changing his ſcheme, but ſteddily

steddily adheres to the principles of craft and villany to the last. When he found himself to be discovered, and all his schemes broke, yet he is so far from repenting and renouncing his former dishonesty, that he trusts entirely to his own wicked invention to bring himself off, and resolves to cover all he had done, by a deeper fraud and artifice. And this method is not only consistent with itself, but is most likely to succeed. The surest way to prosper in dishonest courses is by determining at once to lay aside all scruples, and go all lengths. Most persons are dishonest by halves: will commit one fraud, or utter one falshood, yet boggle at another. But this is stopping short in the road, and acting weakly and inconsistently. It seldom happens that one lie does not require another to support it; and one fraud a second to cover it. Where the foundation is laid in fraud and falshood, endless artifices must be used to support the building; or it will be in imminent danger of falling upon the builder's head,

head, and overwhelming him in the ruins. When men are once entered into the crooked ways of iniquity, they soon become so entangled and bewildered, that they find it almost impossible to retreat, and are under a sort of necessity of proceeding; especially if they would reap the advantage of it, and arrive at the end proposed. The scheme of iniquity must be pursued steddily and diligently, in order to reap the benefit of it, or enjoy ease and security in it. To this end, the first qualification requisite is to subdue conscience, and not suffer it to interfere, lest it should disconcert your measures, or hinder you in pursuing the right plan of operations. But beside this, many extraordinary qualifications are very necessary. It is not for a fool to hope for success in this way. He ought to have great abilities—an excellent memory—a head full of invention—a large circumspection—and a long foresight;—not so far indeed as to look to another world; but as far as ever his affairs in this world extend,

extend, and no further. Without some such rare talents, though he had ever so hearty a desire to grow rich by knavery, he would in all probability miss of his aim, and reduce himself to infamy and ruin. The steward in the parable escaped but narrowly; only by the help of a good judgment and ready invention, as well as perseverance in iniquity.

We shall now proceed to consider, in the third place, the application of the foregoing parable which our Savior makes to his own disciples.—It is not difficult to assign some probable reasons, why our Savior selected the character of an unjust steward to be exhibited to his audience. All men who are possessed of any share of worldly substance, should consider themselves not as absolute proprietors and masters of their wealth; but rather as stewards, entrusted with it by divine providence, and accountable for the use of it to the supreme lord and proprietor of the world. Beside, the disciples

disciples of our Savior were intended by him for a much more important office and trust, than could arise from the amplest possession of wealth. For they were intended to be, as the apostle expresses it, *Stewards of the divine mysteries, and of the manifold grace of God.* Hence our Savior argues with them in consequence of the preceding parable, *If ye have not been faithful in the unrighteous Mammon, who will commit to your trust the true riches?* Stiling those spiritual powers and endowments, with which he intended to entrust them, *the true riches,* in contrast to worldly possessions, which are of a false and deceitful nature. And again, *If ye are not faithful in that which is another's, who will give unto you that which shall be your own?*—The internal endowments of the mind are alone properly denominated *men's own:* all external things are only *lent them* for their present use, and management; and may be at any time taken from them. If then the disciples were dishonest stewards of their worldly possessions,

possessions, whether larger or smaller; how could he entrust them with the knowledge of truth, or impart to them those virtues, which, whoever is possessed of, may stile his own? Or how could they be qualified for those treasures in heaven which would be their own for ever? How small a share of wealth soever they were possessed of; yet if they were dishonest in these little affairs, it would prove them to be wholly unfit for greater. A dishonest mind would utterly disqualify them for the high office of being his apostles; which required a perfect integrity, and a mind superior to all worldly motives. *He that is faithful in that which is least, is faithful also in much: and he that is unjust in the least is unjust also in much.* i. e. The same unjust disposition and worldly affection, which tempt men to fraud and treachery in little and temporal affairs, will operate also in greater, in those of a spiritual nature and the utmost importance. Consequently such persons were by no means qualified for the purpose he intended.

ed. We have a memorable example to this effect, even in one of his disciples, *Judas*; who probably was present at the time, and on whom he had *his eye* in particular: for he was *our Savior's steward*, and was tempted by his hpyocritical and covetous spirit, first to follow him in hopes of wealth and preferment; and when disappointed of that, then to defraud him (which he had opportunity to do by bearing the purse) and at last to betray him to death, for the sake of a bribe offered him by the pharisees and chief priests. Thus he who was at first unjust in a little, was at last guilty of the most aggravated treachery. But the other disciples, who were of a sincere and honest disposition in their worldly affairs, became afterwards faithful apostles of CHRIST, and *intitled* to the incorruptible riches of his kingdom, which he hath given them, and which shall be their own for ever.

Now to consider in the fourth place, how far the scribes and pharisees were interested
in

in and affected by the foregoing parable and subsequent exhortations. There is too much reason to apprehend, that they rather resembled *Judas* in their temper and conduct than the other disciples: and that, as the prodigal son in the foregoing parable was designed to represent the publicans and sinners; so the character of the scribes and pharisees is exhibited, in some measure at least, in that of the unjust steward. So far were they from being in reality, what they hypocritically assumed to be, the just men who need no repentance. Covetousness, fraud, dissimulation, and cunning, are the chief ingredients which compose the character of the men of this world. And we find by the whole tenor of the gospel history, that these were the distinguished qualities of the scribes and pharisees. How far they might insinuate themselves into the esteem and confidence of other people by their solemn deportment and religious appearances, we cannot particularly and minutely ascertain.

But

But it is evident, that they were held in veneration by the common people: and probable, that by becoming *trustees* of pulic charities, *executors* of wills, and *receivers* of gifts to pious uses, they found means and opportunity of *devouring widow's houses*, and practising various frauds for their own emolument. The picture then of the unjust steward, tho' perhaps not applicable to each of them in every point, yet had so much in general of their likeness in it, as was sufficient to alarm them. And the evangelist expressly says, *The pharisees, who were covetous, heard these things, and they derided him.* But what motive or pretence could they possibly have to deride him; if they had not secretly applied the character to themselves, and understood the whole discourse as levelled at them, though indirectly. It is plain that it galled their consciences, and raised their spleen and indignation. And therefore in return, dissembling the real motive of resentment, they put on looks of scorn and derision,

endeavored

endeavored to repay him with infult, and affected to treat his doctrine with fovereign contempt.

Upon this, when he found, that they had not only refifted the admirable pleas he had made ufe of in his own vindication, but difcovered their malignity of temper on account of his admonitions againft fraud and avarice; he refolves to throw off all referve, and charges them in direct terms, *Ye are they who juftify yourfelves before men; who deceive the world with your folemn and fpecious appearances. But God knoweth your hearts. For that which is high amongft men, is often low and deteftable in the fight of God.*

Thus it always is with difhoneft minds. The ftronger the arguments are, which are ufed againft them, the more they are determined to make refiftance, to triumph in a conceit of themfelves, and a contempt of thofe who pretend to inftruct them. Men may be reclaimed, like *the prodigal son*, from all other vices, provided there is an ingenuity and sensibility of mind remaining. But a fraudulent villanous temper, like that of the *unjust steward*, is proof against every thing. None are so incapable of true wisdom, as persons of a low and selfish cunning: none so insusceptible of repentance and amendment, as the dishonest and treacherous. *It is easier to make a camel to pass through the eye of a needle*, than to convert a hypocrite to honesty. He has always a subterfuge in the hollows of his own heart, where he skulks secure, and bids defiance to all the attacks of reason and religion. Here lies his wisdom and his strength: to this he trusts at all times: by this, he hopes to deceive the world, conquer all opposition, accomplish his own ends, and establish his own interest.

The same temper will lead him to act in like manner, in regard to God and his own conscience. By his own craft he will *impose upon himself*; and flatter himself with the delusive hope of escaping with impunity in the day of final account. He will presume, that the same artifice, by which he has perverted his own judgment, will pass with the omniscient Lord and Judge of the world: and will hope to save himself by a plea similar to that of *Lord, Lord, have I not prophesied in thy name?*— till he shall hear to his utter confusion, *Depart from me, ye that work iniquity.*

DISCOURSE VI.

Of the subtle Steward, or hardened Villain.

Luke xvi. 8.

For the children of this world are in their generation wiser than the children of light.

THIS reflexion of our *Savior* is introduced by the preceding ſtory of a fraudulent ſteward; who inſtead of improving his maſter's eſtates, had waſted them: and when required to give an account of his conduct, inſtead of making any ſatisfaction, contrives by an accumulated fraud, to procure himſelf friends at his maſter's expence. His lord, whatever reſentments he might have of his ſervant's diſhoneſty and treachery, yet could not forbear acknowledging, that he had acted a politic part, and had taken the moſt artful and effectual method to gain friends and to secure to himself an immediate support. From this supposed instance of dishonest policy, our Savior draws this general observation, *That the children of this world are wiser in their generation than the children of light.*

Let us inquire, I. into the meaning; II. the truth; and, III. the use of this observation or apotheme spoke by our Lord on the foregoing occasion.

I. The meaning of it.—It cannot be imagined, that his intention was to give any encouragement or commendation to those dishonest artifices, by which men sometimes obtain their worldly ends. Nothing can be more inconsistent with the conduct of our Savior, and the spirit of all his discourses. And it may be proper to observe, that the word in the original, translated *wiser*, means in the strict sense, more thoughtful and sagacious, more attentive to the ends they have in view, and more

more artful and steddy in pursuing them. It is applicable either to a good or ill design, to an honest or dishonest policy. Thus the lord commended the unjust steward, because he had done, in this sense of the word, *wisely:* and our Savior uses the same term, when he recommends it to his disciples, to be *wise as serpents,* and at the same time *harmless as doves.*

The term *prudence,* in English, is nearly of the same ambiguous import. In the proper and legitimate sense of the word, it implies true wisdom and a sound judgment. It is the presiding intelligence, which controuls all the affections and desires, and directs the virtues of the heart in their operation. But in another and illegitimate sense, it is mere craft and selfishness. One who has the character of a very prudent man, is often at the bottom a very cunning and self-interested man. Under a pretence of acting prudently, men become downright hypocrites—flatter and deceive others—monopolize

monopolize and defraud in trade—*sell* themselves or their children in marriage—betray their friends or their country—make shipwreck of faith and a good conscience—to serve their own interest.

By the *children of this world* are evidently meant worldly-minded persons, whose hopes and designs all terminate upon external possessions: and by the appellation of *the children of light*, are distinguished all those, whose views are of a higher nature; and who prefer the advantages of virtue, and the rewards of it hereafter, to all other acquisitions. Our Savior's denominating persons of these opposite characters, the children of this world, and the children of light, is agreeable to the usual language of the holy Scripture. And the same manner of expression is to this day in common use in some southern nations.

The sense of the text then appears to be this: that the men of this world, whose
only

only aim and purpose in life is to lay hold of and secure to themselves worldly possessions, use more attention and contrivance in compassing their ends, than the men of virtue and religion in obtaining the objects of their view: or are more ingenious and industrious to provide for this life, than the other to lay hold of eternal life.—He adds, that we might be more certain of his meaning, are wiser *in their generation*, *i. e.* in their sphere of action, or the present scene: considering the narrow compass they take into their view, and that all their schemes are confined to the little scene of this life; and setting aside the comparative meanness and insignificance of the objects they propose to themselves; the men of this world are wiser than those of another, or excel them in point of attention and foresight, of art and application, in the prosecution of the ends they aim at.

Having thus endeavored to fix the *meaning* of our Savior's observation, let us proceed

proceed, II. to enquire into the *truth* of it. For though we may safely rely on his authority for the truth of every thing he has asserted; this kind of implicit faith will not thorowly answer the purpose of his instructions. For in order to make them most useful to us, we ought to examine them, to see the truth and feel the weight of what he hath said, and make his reflections in some measure our own. He knew, say the evangelists, what was in man: *i. e.* he understood human nature; and his observation resulted from a perfect knowledge of mankind. In order then to make a due application of it, we must enter into the same kind of knowledge, understand something of the ways of men, and mark their views and purposes in the transactions of life, and the methods they take to accomplish them. Not that any profound penetration or uncommon degree of experience is necessary: we may be sufficiently apprized of the truth of the proposition in the text, without prying

far

far into the myfteries of iniquity, and difcovering all the wiles and ftratagems thro' which men purfue their feveral objects of pleafure, profit, and preferment. Befide, an honeft and ingenuous mind finds no pleafure in fuch fpeculations, and is not defirous of being let into the fecrets of wickednefs, or founding the depths of Satan. A knowledge of this kind is rather painful to him, and he will defire no more of it, than is fufficient for his own defence againft the artifices of ill-defigning men. It may be fufficient to our conviction, to obferve in general, the prudence and induftry of the men of the world, in purfuit of their fole or favorite object, wealth: and without confidering the honefty or difhonefty of the methods they ufe; the point of our prefent attention is, the abilities they exert, or the worldly wifdom they difcover.—And here, to pafs over the numberlefs fchemes and projects that have been formed, the fruit of much thought and wonderful invention; the more ufual and ordinary

ordinary courfe of affairs will afford fcope enough for our obfervation.

Mark the fons of worldly care and bufinefs—fee how much they excel in every property of that wifdom we fpeak of—how ftudious—how inquifitive—how artful—and how fteddy!

First, they are fteddy to their own purpofe, true to their own caufe. Their object is their own intereft, and they keep it always in view. All their words and actions are intended to be directly or indirectly fubfervient to that one point. The great purpofe of their lives is to get wealth: they look therefore upon all things and perfons around them, as tools which they are to prepare and make ufe of in the execution of that defign: and they never fuffer themfelves to be diverted from it: they are averfe to all ftudies or enterprizes that are not fome way or other connected with it: this is the only fcience they defire to be inftructed in: every thing is neglected that is not, every thing attended to that is conducive to this end: and they purfue it, not at certain times only, or on fpecial occafions, but with unremitting conftancy, and to the laft moment of life. Here is fteddinefs—this is application and perfeverance.

(2.) THEY are exceedingly thoughtful—their heads are often at work, when other men's are idle—they forecaft the event, lay plans, compare different methods, reject this and prefer the other as more effectual—they feek for information, aim at the beft intelligence, keep fufpicion awake, are always upon guard, left they fhould be furprized and overreached, and look with an eye of penetration upon every perfon with whom they tranfact bufinefs. And when the paffion for wealth is heightened into the dotage of avarice, what concern, what fear, what anxious thought and perpetual contrivance to fecure or increafe what they have got! *They fit up late, and rife early, and eat the bread of carefulnefs.*

(3.) THEY

(3.) THEY excel in zeal also. The worshippers of Mammon surpass all men in a sincere ardor of affection to the object of their devotion. *They say to gold, Thou art my hope, and to fine gold, Thou art my confidence:* And they say it from the bottom of their hearts. Wealth is their god, and they have no other god before him; and they love him with all their heart and soul and mind and strength. Their affections are never estranged from him, and they have hardly the least esteem for any other thing. When he smiles upon them with the light of his countenance, *i. e.* when they have a prospect of great gain, what joy does it infuse into their hearts! What a secret pleasure and alacrity does the conscious sense of it give them! But if he frown upon them, what dejection and grief, what sincere mourning and lamentation! Their GOD has forsaken them; and miserable as they are, what shall they do?—Their only resource is, with all submission and diligence to seek his favor yet again;

again; and if, like the steward in the parable, they cannot dig, and are ashamed to beg, any method will be taken, honest or dishonest, provided it appears effectual to the purpose. Nothing moves men of this character, nothing touches them to the heart, but what relates to their interest. They are cold and indifferent to all other subjects: and tho' you were to speak on the weightiest subject with the eloquence of an angel, your words would be to them only as a pleasant sound of one that plays well on an instrument; but a sound which in their ears has no sense or meaning. But in what concerns their interest, how quick of apprehension—how sensibly affected—then they are rouzed and all awake—their passions rise—they are animated and transported.——Here is zeal—this is the enthusiasm of that sect, which our Savior stiles, *the children of this world.*

(4.) It may be proper to observe also how artful and inventive they are.—Beside the common and beaten road of life, how many by-ways of their own finding out in order to compass their ends——And when pressed with any difficulty, what fetches and evasions, what duplicity of language and conduct; and like a certain sagacious animal, how skilful to lay traces to amuse and deceive, or to gain some covert and subterfuge!——The steward in the parable had lived splendidly upon the plunder of his master's fortunes; and for a time had the art to conceal his frauds: But when they were detected, and that he found he could hold his post no longer, and must give in his accompts; it might be thought, that he had run to his utmost length, and had entangled himself effectually. And indeed he seems to be terribly disconcerted.——*What shall I do? My lord taketh from me the stewardship—I cannot dig—to beg I am ashamed.* But making use again of his invention, he found a notable expedient still remaining, by which he could extricate himself from the present difficulty; and make

make some provision for his future subsistence; and losing no time, puts it immediately in execution.

LASTLY, They admire this science of worldly wisdom, delight in the study and practice of it, and esteem it the highest attainment of the human understanding; and for this reason make a greater proficiency in it. Learning they look upon as a poor accomplishment—honesty, a vulgar quality—generosity, a meer bait to catch applause—and all those virtues which constitute real worth, as of little value. They hold such persons in no esteem, and give them no praise: Or if they are obliged to express some approbation, take care to throw in an equal mixture of detraction. At the same time they value themselves excessively for their own wisdom——are pleased above measure with the success of their schemes—and exult with a conscious superiority over those who are less skilled in the artifices of mankind, and the crafty

management

management of affairs. They defpife the men of fimplicity and plain-dealing, who dully purfue the ftraight and open road of life, and laugh in fecret at thofe whom they can impofe upon; but envy thofe who are more fagacious and fuccefsful than themfelves; and are excited by a fpirit of emulation to improve in the arts of life, and to furpafs all their neighbors in worldly acquifitions. Hence they excel, and *are wifer in their generation than the children of light.*

LET us now turn our attention to the men of a different character, whom our Savior diftinguifhes by the title of *the children of light*; and compare their genius, fkill and application in purfuit of their ends, with the ability of the men of the former character. There are, no doubt, (our Savior plainly fuppofes that there are) fome men in the world, who amidft all their fecular cares and purfuits, aim at fomething befide the things of this world, and

and something beyond the bounds of this life; who prefer the internal possession of innocence and virtue to external treasures; and who actually believe, that there will be another life; and think themselves obliged by the highest motives to make some provision for it. The objects of their peculiar attention and pursuit, are wisdom and virtue, exerted in a worthy and useful conduct; as the foundation of peace, stability, and satisfaction of mind in this world, and of eternal life and happiness hereafter. And did they pursue these truly valuable and desirable objects with equal spirit, as the men of this world pursue riches; what success and prosperity would attend them! and what encomiums would they justly merit!——

But a proper knowledge of mankind will convince us, that our Savior's assertion is continually verified in human life. How much nobler soever those ends are, which the men of religion professedly aim at, at, than those which the children of this world propose to themselves, the latter far surpass the former, in a sagacious and diligent attention to them. Religion is practised, and the everlasting treasures and felicities of another world pursued, with indifference and negligence, compared to the intense care and application employed in worldly affairs. If some men were to mind religion as much as others do the world, and were as thoughtful and solicitous to grow wise, as others to become rich, as studious and ingenious to do good, as others to get gain; what improvements might be expected? and what happy fruits would be produced from such noble and singular exertions of skill and industry? But were we to search through the whole world, and to select out of it men of the best characters, could we hope to find any among them, who are as much in earnest to obtain the rewards of virtue and religion, and as wise in taking the most effectual means, as many are to secure and increase

their

their temporal poffeffions? The contrary is too apparent: and nothing occurs more frequently to our obfervation than the weaknefs, negligence, and errors of good men, their want of judgment, or attention, or refolution, or diligence, in the practice of religion. How often are they diverted by temptations from purfuing the ends they propofe? How eafily impofed upon by defigning men? How flow in profecution of what they profeffedly aim at, and carelefs of finding out the true means of obtaining it?—It may raife our admiration to fee the art and induftry of fome men in their worldly affairs, and to procure wealth: But to fee good men employing equal degrees of attention and activity in the practice of religion, in guarding againft errors, in liftening to information, in carrying on ufeful defigns, in beftowing their time and their wealth to the beft purpofes, and providing for their eternal intereft and happinefs—would be a much more uncommon fpectacle.

The natural cause which may be assigned of this great difference, is, the different nature and situation of the several objects. For the things of another world lie beyond our sight and experience—and virtue, and the happiness of it, are objects of our reason and understanding, but cannot captivate our senses and passions as worldly things usually do. And therefore, tho' men may prefer the former to the latter in their calm and deliberate judgment; yet cool judgment, or mere belief, has but a feeble influence, compared to the warm and vigorous affections of a worldly heart, especially when increased by indulgence and enflamed by success.

Let us now proceed, Thirdly, to the use we ought to make of the observation in the text.——The first point of true wisdom is to fix upon right ends or objects to be pursued in the conduct of life. The second, to employ our abilities in a prosecution of those ends.——It is in the first and

and leading point, that the men of this world are widely miftaken. They place their fupreme good in external poffeffions. They conceive nothing greater and happier than worldly profperity, to be, and to be reputed, rich, and continually encreafing in wealth, and to enjoy the fuperiority and affluence which attend large and growing poffeffions. They confider not the precarioufnefs and emptinefs of thefe things. They know not the dignity and value of true virtue, or the honor and happinefs which it beftows. They are infenfible of the pleafures of a generous mind; and the elevated views, the pleafing hopes, the folid confidence, which true religion infpires. With all their prudence and forefight, they fee but a little way before them; never think of the condition they may find themfelves in after death; and are deftitute of all fenfe and confideration in the moft momentous concern of life. They imagine themfelves *to be rich and encreafed in goods, and to have need of nothing, and know not that*

that they are poor, and naked, and blind, and miserable. But in the second or subsequent point of wisdom they excell, and are wiser in their generation than the children of light. Allowing them their first principles, and that the worldly ends and objects they aim at are as valuable as they imagine them to be, and that their highest interest and happiness lies in them; if we allow them these premises, they are right in the consequence, and deserve to be applauded for their skill and assiduity, which they often discover in pursuing them. The lord commended the unjust steward because he had done wisely. The fault does not lie in the ability or diligence men exert; but in the dishonest or indirect methods they are tempted to use in order to obtain such things, and their neglect of things infinitely better. Men may pursue the world with all the sagacity and diligence they are masters of: such conduct is generally commended, and reason does not disapprove it; nor does our holy religion forbid it, as

far

far as is confiftent with the rules of honor, and integrity, with the good of fociety, and with a fupreme view to their own eternal intereft and happinefs. But when men make gain their religion, enflave themfelves to Mammon, and perfer his fervice to the fervice of God; then prudence degenerates into craft, induftry is worfe than idlenefs, and all their worldly wifdom becomes in effect the greateft folly. Judgment, penetration, fkill, care, forecaft, and induftry, are qualities of great ufe and importance: for without them, no valuable end can be purfued, or poffeffion acquired. But thefe qualities, though excellent in themfelves, may be all employed to low ends and unworthy purpofes, in purfuits that will terminate in no advantage either to ourfelves or others, or in accomplifhing felfifh, avaritious, and unjuft defigns, to the hurt of others, and to our own eternal perdition.— It may juftly move our regret, to fee admirable talents proftituted to mean and ignoble ends: to obferve men indefatigable in in acquiring what will do them no good, exceedingly bufy in trifling affairs, wonderfully ingenious to no valuable purpofe, and employing their utmoft thought and activity, when the principal effect of all, is to indulge the paffion, and feed the growing difeafe, of covetoufnefs,—to make themfelves mifers in this world, and in another, miferable or nothing.

On the other hand, the children of light fee things in a different view, take a clearer and more extenfive profpect, difcern the objects which religion propofes, and acknowledge the fovereign dignity, excellence, and worth of them. They are therefore right in their principles, and wife in the firft and capital point of wifdom: but unhappily fail in the fubfequent point; and fuffer themfelves to be far outdone by the children of this world, in a judicious and affiduous application. This is their reproach: tho' they feek for glory, honor, and immortality; they feek with indolence, inattention,

inattention, and imprudence, in comparison of the sagacious judgment, the keen inspection, and the patient continuance, with which men follow after the precarious possessions of this mortal life.

The instruction our Savior intended to convey to us is, that we take example from the men of this world, and imitate their policy, prudence, and diligence; but with a view to greater and worthier objects than those which engross the whole attention of these sons of earth.—It is an elegant epithet which he applies to riches—he stiles them unrighteous, not respecting the means by which they are sometime obtained, but the very nature and quality of them; implying that there is a knavery and deceit in them—they delude and disappoint men——they carry flattering appearances, but there is nothing substantially good and lasting in them. Mammon promises men great things, and a world of happiness; but he was a liar from the beginning, and ought not to be be trufted. Some men efteem him as their beft friend: but he frequently proves treacherous and cruel, often betrays them to their hurt, and always deferts at the laft.

HEAR then the important advice of our blefled Savior: *Make to yourfelves friends of the Mammon of unrighteoufnefs*; fo ufe and improve the fleeting and deceitful riches of this world, that when death fhall difpoflefs you of them, and eject you from your prefent poffeffions and dwellings, you may be received into everlafting habitations.— To this end, let us be as wife to do good, and to become rich in goodnefs, as other men are to become rich in worldly goods: for hereby we fhall lay up for ourfelves *treafures in heaven, where no thief approacheth, nor ruft corrupteth.*

Happy is the man that findeth this wifdom, and with all his getting getteth this underftanding. For the merchandize of it is better than the merchandize of filver, and the gain thereof than fine gold.

DISCOURSE VII.

Of the inhuman rich *Jew*, and his Brethren.

Luke xvi. from 19. to the end.

There was a certain rich man, which was cloathed in purple and fine linen, and fared sumptuously every day. And there was a certain beggar named Lazarus, which was laid at his gate full of sores; and desiring to be fed with the crumbs which fell from the rich man's table: moreover the dogs came and licked his sores. And it came to pass that the beggar died; and was carried by the angels into Abraham's bosom. The rich man also died and was buried. And in hell he lift up his eyes, being in torments, and seeth Abraham afar off, and Lazarus in his bosom. And he cried, and said, Father Abraham, have mercy on me; and send Lazarus, that he may dip the tip of his finger in water, and cool my tongue: for I am tormented in this flame. But

Abraham said, Son, remember, that thou in thy life-time receivedst thy good things, and likewise Lazarus evil things: but now he is comforted, and thou art tormented. And besides all this, between us and you there is a great gulf fixed: so that they which would pass from hence to you, cannot; neither can they pass to us, that would come from thence. Then he said, I pray thee, therefore, father, that thou wouldest send him to my father's house: for I have five brethren; that he may testify unto them, lest they also come into this place of torment. Abraham saith unto him, They have Moses and the prophets, let them hear them. And he said, Nay, father Abraham; but if one went unto them from the dead, they will repent. And he said unto him, If they hear not Moses and the prophets, neither will they be persuaded, though one rose from the dead.

AS this parable hath a manifest reference to the Jews, to the wealthier

thier part of them, and to such as rejected our Savior; so we cannot suppose any audience or occasion more proper for it, than the same which gave rise to the foregoing parables. They may be considered as following each other in a proper series.

His former representations being ineffectual to the conviction of the pharisees and scribes; he makes use of stronger images, more striking contrasts, and more affecting incidents; and puts his sentiments into the mouth of their great ancestor *Abraham*, for whom they had a high veneration, and from whom they were proud of being descended. He extends his scenery also to another world. The scene of some of his parables is wholly in this world; of others, wholly in the future state: In this, there is a transition from one to the other.

We shall (1.) give a narration of the parable: (2.) shew the propriety of it, as addressed to the pharisees and scribes: and (3.) make

(3.) make obfervations on the feveral parts of it.

(1.) THE Parable.

THERE was a certain rich *Jew*, who feemed from his manner of life, to confider the wealth he was poffeffed of, only as the means of procuring to himfelf whatever might gratify his own inclinations; and to apply it to no other purpofe. His whole ftudy was to pleafe his fancy and appetites, with the moft exquifite refinements of luxury: and his higheft ambition, to make a fumptuous and fplendid appearance. Thefe things engroffed his heart and affections: and hence his temper became fo felfifh and contracted, that he had loft all fentiments of humanity and beneficence; and had no conception of thofe tender fympathies, which lead men to compaffionate the miferable, and relieve the neceffitous.

AT this man's gate was laid (left there perhaps by thofe who were grown weary

or

or incapable of taking care of him) a poor *Jew*, named *Lazarus*, in the greatest distress, and ready to perish through the extremities of disease and want. Unable to subsist by his own industry, he was of necessity thrown upon the kindness of others. And in hopes, that where there was so much affluence he might find some relief, as a kind of last resource, he rested his fate on the humanity of this his opulent neighbor. He concluded, that a case so deplorable as his was, could not fail of exciting the compassion of a fellow creature, a neighbor, and brother *Jew*; especially as all he desired or presumed to hope for were the crumbs which fell from his table. The poor man however was disappointed even in this slender hope. Not the least notice is taken of the piteous spectacle by any of the family: the same spirit of selfishness and voluptuousness prevailed through every part of it, and extinguished the sense of humanity and compassion. He was left to struggle with all the variety of wretchedness,

wretchedness, till encreasing pain and famine put an end to his miserable life.

The apprehension of death is often bitter to those who live in ease and prosperity: But how friendly and acceptable must the approach of it be to him, whose condition was so forlorn and hopeless! It was indeed a most desirable change; as it proved, not only the end of all his sufferings, but the commencement of his happiness. From a death attended with the most abject and distresful circumstances, he was raised to another life, was conducted by angels to the habitation of the blessed, and placed there in one of its highest mansions, even next to his great ancestor *Abraham*.

The rich man also died.—Free from the pains of a lingering distemper, he might sink at once from the full of enjoyment of life and health into the sleep of death. He was buried too, and, no doubt, with a pomp and magnificence becoming the wealth and splendor in which he had lived.

But

But what a sad reverse did death prove to him! the period of his pleasures, and the beginning of his sufferings.—Though while living, and in the midst of his mirth and dissipation, he might never think of his latter end; or might suppose, that his existence would cease with his life, and futurity be no more to him, than if he had never been born; or flatter himself with a hope that his *Jewish* descent and religious profession would suffice to exempt him from punishment, and entitle him to a place with his blessed ancestors—he awakes in the midst of torments:——And in that dreadful situation, throwing his eyes about him for relief or escape, to his extreme astonishment and confusion, he discovers, at a remote distance, the great father of his nation, and *Lazarus* by his side. For a moment, the remembrance of his cruel neglect of the wretched *Lazarus*, a fear of his resentment, and an awe of so illustrious a personage as *Abraham*, intimidated and held him in suspense. But seeing none other to apply to in his anguish, and hoping that he might possibly obtain some relief, from the kindness and compassion of those happy spirits, after a violent struggle between hope and despair, and stimulated by the acuteness of his pain, he ventured to address his progenitor, and implore mercy. But conscious how unworthy he was of mercy, who had been wont to shew none, all the favor he thought fit to ask, was the least abatement of his misery even but for a moment—*a drop of water only upon his tongue—from the finger of Lazarus.*

THE good *patriarch* no sooner heard his request, than with the serenity and benignity of a celestial spirit, he first intimated to him the justice of the case, by reminding him of the different conditions, in which he and *Lazarus* had lived upon earth: and then alledged the impossibility of a compliance. " Remember, Son" (said he) "the
" goods which you enjoyed, and the evils
" which he suffered. As it was not fit
" that

"that difference should continue for e-
"ver;—the scene is now reversed——you
"have exchanged conditions—he is com-
"forted, and you are tormented. Beside
"all this, you ask for what is impossible—
"each of us are confined within our pro-
"per spheres—the great boundaries of the
"different regions we inhabit are impass-
"able, and prevent all intercourse."

HUMBLE and earnest then as the petition was, it could not be granted him. And the unhappy criminal, silenced by an argument so convincing, forbore all further solicitation in his own behalf. But that he might not lose all advantage from this interview with *Abraham*, his next thought was of his surviving brethren. He knew so much of their manner of life, as to have painful apprehensions of the consequence. And though his own condition was hopeless and without remedy, he had so much love for them, and felt so strong a desire of preventing, if possible, their final misery,

fery, that he earneſtly interceded for them. His intreaty was, "*That* as *Lazarus* could not come to his relief, he might be ſent to his brethren on earth, to warn them effectually of their danger, leſt they alſo ſhould come into the ſame place of torment."——But in this petition he was equally unſucceſsful. The *patriarch* anſwered; "There is no reaſon for having recourſe to ſuch uncommon means of reformation—the admonitions they have already are ſufficient, if they will give heed to them—they have *Moſes* and the *prophets*, let them hear them."——This reply did not convince or ſatisfy the ſuppliant. Perſuaded of the efficacy of his expedient, and that tho' ordinary means might fail, ſo extraordinary a method would certainly produce a good effect;—he urged his ſuit with a degree of confident importunity: "Nay, Father *Abraham*, but if one went unto them from the dead, they will repent."—The wiſe *patriarch* thought differently; and concluded the converſation with

with peremptorily assuring him, "That
" whatever success he might expect from
" such an expedient, it would prove in-
" effectual: and that if they would pay
" no regard to *Moses* and *the prophets*, nei-
" ther would they be persuaded, no, not
" though one arose from the dead."

We are now to consider the propriety of this parable, as addressed to the pharisees and scribes.—The principal or concluding point of it appears to be a prediction of their final unbelief, impenitence, and condemnation, notwithstanding the strongest evidence and admonition which would be afforded them.—We should consider this prediction as comprehending not every individual of that party of his audience, but only the generality or greater part of them; and as a conclusion drawn from moral premises, rather than a prophecy, resulting from absolute prescience, or founded on physical certainty. As the patriarch infers concerning the five brethren,

thren, from their total difregard to *Moſes* and the *prophets*, that neither would they be perſuaded or converted, tho' one aroſe from the dead; ſo our Lord intended to infer the aforementioned prediction concerning the phariſees and ſcribes, from the conduct and diſpoſition which they diſcovered in their oppoſition to him;—not merely from the oppoſition itſelf, but that malignity of heart from which it proceeded.

Particularly, in the firſt place, their covetous, unjuſt, fraudulent and hypocritical diſpoſition; which he expoſes in the character of the unjuſt ſteward, and the ſubſequent inſtructions, addreſſed indeed to his own diſciples, but pointed at them. For they were men of this world, and very wiſe in their generation, very artful in preſerving exterior appearances, and ſupporting a reputation in the opinion of the vulgar, without any real integrity or worth. Under the moſt ſpecious maſk of ceremonious

nious gravity and sanctity, and of a zealous attachment to religion, they gratified their own avarice, and obtained their worldly ends; *devouring widow's houses, and for a pretence,* or disguise, *making long prayers.*— In the next place, their luxury and inhumanity—which are intimated in the condition and conduct of the rich man in this parable. They made indeed the like pretences to charity as they did to devotion. For they gave alms publickly at certain stated times and by sound of trumpet. But as in this case, not the most impotent and needy, the most modest and deserving, but rather the most able and active, the most forward and importunate beggars would be likely to share all the benefit of such alms, so it was meant as a mere parade or pompous show of generosity, by which they threw a cloke over their real inhumanity and neglect of such as were in the greatest distress and most deserving of their compassion. It was sufficient they thought to vindicate their total neglect of the poorest and

and most distressed object, though a brother-*Jew*, if they could stile him a publican or a sinner. With what haughtiness and contempt do they reply to the poor beggar who had been miraculously cured of his native blindness by our *Savior*, when he presumed to defend the character of his benefactor, *Thou wast altogether born in sin; and dost thou teach us?* They made the like pretences also to fasting and abstemiousness: But though they might really observe some stated times of fasting, yet it was for the most part only *disfiguring their faces, that they might appear unto men to fast*: for they *loved the uppermost rooms at feasts,* where we may presume they did not mean to give specimens of their abstinence. And when they made a feast, they took care to invite only their rich friends and neighbors, who could make them a recompence, and at whose tables they could amply repay themselves by a luxurious indulgence.——And in the third place, their real contempt of the law and the prophets, *i. e.* of the most important

important moral precepts and inftructions of that religion which they profeffed. One part of their charge againft him was, that he taught things contrary, not only to the traditions of the elders (which was true in fome inftances, becaufe they made void the commandments of GOD by their traditions) but alfo to *the law and the prophets*; which was not true. For he was a perfect example of all that righteoufnefs which the law and the prophets required; and by his inftructions explained and enforced the feveral important branches of the law. Yet under color of their religious zeal, they traduced him as a fubverter of the law and the prophets. This is probably the reafon, though it is not expreffed by the hiftorian, of the paffage preceding this parable.—*The law and the prophets were until John. Since that time the kingdom of G O D is preached, and every man preffeth into it. But it is eafier for heaven and earth to pafs away, than for one tittle of the law to fail. Whofoever putteth away his wife, and marrieth another,*

ther, committeth adultery: and whosoever marrieth her that is put away from her husband, committeth adultery. Which passage appears to be meant in answer to the popular objection which they had raised against him, that he set up his own authority in opposition to that of Moses and the prophets: as a proof of which they alledged his denying the right of repudiation. He therefore plainly intimates to them, " That John the Bap-
" tist and himself had an authority equal
" to that of the preceding prophets; that
" the kingdom of GOD, which they preached
" and urged men to embrace, was not
" subversive but promotive of the main end
" and design of the law of GOD, which was
" of immutable obligation, and as fixed as
" the constitution of nature itself; and that
" as to the instance of repudiation, he con-
" sidered it as no part of the law, but an un-
" reasonable licence, productive of immoral
" consequences." In other places he clearly defines what he meant by *the law and the prophets,* which he asserts that he came *not to destroy but to fulfil.* Matth. vii. 7. *Ask and*

it shall be given you: seek and ye shall find: knock and it shall be opened unto you—for your Father in heaven will give good things to them that aſk him——therefore, all things ye would that men ſhould do to you, do ye ſo to them: for this is the law and the prophets. And again, *Thou ſhalt love the Lord thy God with all thy heart, and thy neighbor as thyſelf: On theſe two commandments hang all the law and the prophets.* In this parable he retorts the aforementioned charge which they brought againſt him, by intimating in an admirable manner their real contempt of the law and the prophets, notwithſtanding all their pretended zeal for them: and hence foretells, by the mouth of their great anceſtor *Abraham*, their incorrigible wickedneſs and final miſery, notwithſtanding the moſt powerful means uſed for their conviction and reformation.

THEIR rejection of the goſpel, and implacable enmity to him, did not proceed from any deficiency in the evidence which he offered them; but their immoral difpofitions and incorrigible temper determined them to refift the evidence whatever it was, and to demand continually more and greater.—At one time (Matth. xii. 38.) not leaving it to his wifdom to judge of proper objects and occafions, but prefuming that his miraculous power fhould be exerted at their pleafure, they demanded that a miracle fhould be wrought upon the fpot for their conviction: probably that they might have a pretence, from his refufal, to deny his power, and the truth of the miracles he was faid to have wrought. To this infolent demand he replied, *A wicked and adulterous generation feeketh after a fign: but no fign fhall be given to it, except the fign of the prophet Jonas. For as Jonas was three days and three nights in the fifhes belly, fo fhall the Son of man be three days and three nights in the heart of the earth.* The meaning is, not that he intended to work no more miracles; but that he would not work at their inftance merely, or to gratify their

their curiosity, caprice, or arrogance—but referred them to his own death and resurrection, as the signal proof of his mission.——At another time (Matth. xvi. 1.) after they had seen him work many miracles on earth, they went to him, and with a solemn assurance required him to *shew them a sign from heaven.*——They denied the reality of his miracles, as long as they had any plausible pretence for it. And when they were too numerous and self-evident to admit of a dispute concerning the reality of them; and consequently, the only question left, was concerning the power which wrought them; they roundly asserted that it was not divine but diabolical, and that it proceeded from *Beelzebub the prince of demons:* though they were no less acts of goodness and beneficence, than of power.——When he was hanging upon the cross, they said, *Let him come down from the cross and we will believe in him:* yet when they had the strongest attestations of his being actually risen from the dead; they evaded the force of the evidence, by a moſt abſurd pretence, *that his diſciples had come by night and ſtolen him away:* though they knew that they had themſelves ſecured the ſepulchre, by the ſtrongeſt precautions they could deviſe—a ponderous ſtone to fill up the entrance, joined to the rock by a broad ſeal, and a guard of Roman ſoldiers, who were every one liable to be puniſhed with death, if they ſuffered the ſepulchre to be invaded.

It was not till they had rejected all his admonitions with the utmoſt contempt, and diſcovered an unconquerable prejudice and implacable rancor againſt him, that he openly declaims in the midſt of *Jeruſalem*, and denounces judgment againſt them, (Matth. xxiii.) for their religious profeſſion and wicked practices—*their ſhutting up the kingdom of heaven againſt men, and neither going in themſelves nor ſuffering thoſe that were entring to go in*—*their devouring widow's houſes, and for a pretence making long*

long prayer—their *compassing sea and land to make one proselyte, and making him twofold more the child of hell than themselves*—their *absurd and immoral interpretations of the law*——their *straining at a gnat and swallowing a camel*—*paying tithe of mint, anise and cummin, yet omitting the weightier matters of the law, judgment, mercy, and faith*—their *outwardly appearing righteous unto men, but being within full of hyprocrisy and iniquity, like painted tombs, which appear beautiful outward, but within are full of dead men's bones and of all uncleanness*——their *building the tombs of the prophets and adorning the sepulchres of the righteous, and saying, If we had been in the days of our fathers, we would not have been partakers in the blood of the prophets*; yet making it appear by their own confession as well as conduct, that they were the genuine posterity of them that killed the prophets.——He adds, *Ye fill up then the measure of your fathers. Ye serpents, ye generation of vipers, how can ye escape the damnation of hell?*

THAT he applied the beſt means and arguments in order to remove their prejudices, correct their vices, and work a change in their minds, the foregoing parables afford a clear demonſtration, and are moſt admirable ſpecimens of his manner of conveying inſtruction and reproof. By a careful review of this parable, we may perceive ſomething of that inimitable ſkill, with which he endeavored to work upon the moſt powerful ſprings that actuate human nature, in order to their reformation—upon that ſenſe of humanity, which few are utterly void of—that principle of ſelf-preſervation, which they were undoubtedly poſſeſſed of—that belief of a future ſtate, which they maintained in oppoſition to the ſadducees—that dread of final and remedileſs miſery, which they had too much reaſon to apprehend—that future alarm, which the moſt aſtoniſhing fact of his own reſurrection from the dead (which he here intimates to them) would naturally give them whenever it ſhould come

come to pafs——and confequently, that ftrong jealoufy which they would unavoidably conceive (notwithftanding their evil prejudices) from the whole feries of his difcourfes and tranfactions, left he was in reality their expected *Meffiah*, and his doctrine of divine authority.——His delicacy, in avoiding all defcription of the rich Jew's wicked character, and leaving it to their own reflection, to determine from circumftances, both what it was, and how much like their own——his exquifite manner of introducing their anceftor *Abraham* into the fcene, as the perfon to whom the wretched criminal fues for relief in vain, and who replies to him with fo much propriety and dignity——his making ufe of a character, more refpected than his own by thefe pharifees and fcribes, to give weight to his own fentiments——his touching their national vanity, and converting even that into a motive to their amendment :—— thefe ftrokes would furely be felt by thofe of them who had any ingenuity of mind.

Did not, then, the benevolent Savior of the world afford them sufficient evidence, and apply the fittest means and strongest motives to reform them? Means that would have been effectual, if they had not been invincibly perverse and obstinate, incessantly demanding, with the utmost petulance, more and more evidence? Would he not have been ready to *weep for joy* at so happy an event; as he actually *shed tears of grief* at their incorrigible wickedness, and the calamitous consequences which he foresaw would ensue? For when he drew nigh to *Jerusalem* the last time, and from a neighboring eminence beheld the city, he wept over it, and said, *If thou hadst known, even thou, at least in this thy day, the things which belong unto thy peace! but now they are hid from thine eyes. For the days shall come upon thee, that thine enemies shall cast a trench about thee, and compass thee round, and keep thee in on every side, and shall lay thee even with the ground, and thy children within thee: and they shall not leave in thee one stone upon another:*

another : becaufe thou kneweſt not the time of thy viſitation.——Afterwards, at the temple, and in the midſt of the people, he finiſhed his declamation againſt the phariſees and ſcribes, with theſe words, *O Jeruſalem, Jeruſalem, thou that killeſt the prophets, and ſtoneſt them which are ſent unto thee! how often would I have gathered thy children together, as the hen gathereth her brood under her wings, and ye would not? Behold, your habitation is left unto you deſolate.*——And when, almoſt ſpent with fatigue and cruel treatment, he was conducted through the ſtreets, in order to his crucifixion, and ſaw the tears of them that followed him, he ſaid, *Ye daughters of Jeruſalem, weep not for me, but for yourſelves and for your children :*—as if all his own preſent ſufferings made leſs impreſſion upon his mind, than the ſenſe he had of the miſeries they would be expoſed to!

Now that we may all ſo improve the means

means of the gofpel, as to avoid the fatal confequences of wickednefs and impenitence, and to be found worthy of the mercy and benevolence of the bleffed Savior and Judge of the world, GOD grant of his infinite goodnefs.

DISCOURSE VIII.

Of the inhuman rich *Jew*, and his Brethren.

Luke xvi. from 19. to the end.

There was a certain rich man, which was cloathed in purple and fine linen, and fared sumptuously every day. And there was a certain beggar named Lazarus, which was laid at his gate full of sores; and desiring to be fed with the crumbs which fell from the rich man's table, &c.

WE shall now proceed to make some observations on the structure and several parts of this parable.

It may be thought perhaps by some, that the supposition of a poor man being so abandoned, as to perish in the circumstances here described, is hardly possible. *English* humanity may suggest the ideas of laws

laws made for the relief of the poor, or of hofpitals and infirmaries; and lead us to think fuch a deficiency both of public and private charity very unaccountable. And it is acknowledged, that in this country, including public endowments and private charity, as well as the legal provifion, it is not probable that a cafe fhould occur, fo deplorable as that reprefented in the text, yet remain deftitute of all fuccour. But in moft foreign countries, there is no provifion made by law for the poor; and they are entirely dependent upon the alms of fuch as have the ability and charity to relieve them. Such was the condition of the poor in the land of *Judea* in our Savior's time. The law and the prophets contain indeed many excellent precepts in favor of them, to defend them from the oppreffion, and recommend them to the humanity and bounty of the rich. But if we may form a judgment from many circumftances mentioned in the gofpel-hiftory, fuch precepts were but little obferved by the wealthier fort;

fort; and the whole country seems to have abounded with objects of distress. The indigent, maimed, lame, deaf, blind, diseased, and lunatic, wandered about, seeking relief, or had their several stations where they implored alms. Hence it is, that we find our Savior so frequently exercising his wonderful power and goodness on such miserable objects: and we have reason to believe, that he never refused his miraculous aid, when applied to, provided he found in the person a disposition worthy of such a favor. As to the public alms distributed by the scribes and pharisees, it has been already observed, how little they contributed to the relief of such as were really most needy and wretched.—There is no improbability then in the case described by our Savior, of the poor man who was *laid at the rich man's gate, full of sores, and desiring to be fed with the crumbs which fell from his table.* It was but too natural as well as lively a picture of extreme distress; in which the circumstance added

added of *the dogs coming around him*, is the finishing stroke. Nothing more could be added to move compassion. We may be astonished then at the insensibility of the wealthy man and his domestics, who are supposed to have been spectators of the affecting scene. This must undoubtedly appear to every humane mind as something monstrous and unnatural. For indeed, whatever may be said, even justly, to the disparagement of human nature, it is *not* in our nature to be insensible of the calamities of others; unless a habit of selfishness is previously contracted by indulging to pride, passion, avarice, or voluptuousness. But the rich man, not only was cloathed in purple and fine linen, and fared sumptuously every day; but placed his supreme happiness in these things—These were *his good things*, to which he sacrificed his sense of duty and humanity, and which hardened his heart against the most affecting sight of exquisite distress. He was so puffed up with the pride of wealth, so pampered

pampered with the indulgences of luxury, so devoted to selfish gratifications, as to have lost the natural sense of compassion.

Beside, there was a prevailing notion amongst the *Jews*, which might contribute to his insensibility; as it led them to infer a person's character or qualities from his circumstances, and to misinterpret external calamities into divine judgments; and consequently tended to destroy their sense of humanity. For if we consider the distress any person is reduced to, as in itself a proof of his guilt, and a just punishment from the hand of providence for his former wickedness; we shall certainly feel, if any, the less tenderness and compassion for him. It is to be hoped, that this absurd and barbarous notion obtains no entrance into the minds of Christians. The example of our Savior dying upon the cross, is surely sufficient to teach us to distinguish suffering from sin. But formerly it was very common amongst the *Jews* as well as *Heathens*. Some of our

Savior's disciples were not free from it. For they came to him and told him of the *Galileans*, whose blood *Pilate* had mingled with their sacrifices: to which he replied, knowing their meaning, *Suppose ye that these Galileans were sinners above all the Galileans, because they suffered such things? I tell you, Nay: but except ye repent, ye shall all likewise perish. Or those eighteen, upon whom the tower in Siloam fell, and slew them; think ye that they were sinners above all men that dwelt in Jerusalem? I tell you, Nay: but except ye repent, ye shall all likewise perish.*—— At another time they asked him, *Did this man sin, or his parents, that he was born blind?*——plainly inferring from his being born with that distemper, that there must be some sin as the occasion of it, tho' they knew not where it lay. But he replied, that it was not owing either to any sin of his own, or of his parents.——This language of theirs was too much like that of the pharisees and scribes, when they were examining the poor man, whom our Savior

vior had miraculously cured of his native blindness. For, provoked at the man's presuming to defend the character of his benefactor, in opposition to such respectable persons as themselves, they said, with a contemptuous indignation, *Thou wast altogether born in sin.* By the way, these phrases in scripture, being *born in sin, conceived in sin, brought forth in iniquity, going astray from the mother's womb,* and the like, have a signification very different from the modern phrase of *original sin.* What the *Jews* meant to express, was only the excessive and habitual wickedness of such a particular person, as if his very nature had been perverted from his infancy. The pharisees then pronounced the poor man, *wicked in grain,* as we express it, or from his very cradle, merely because he had the misfortune of being born blind. The rich man then might easily entertain this prejudice against persons in distress: he might be ready to impute the condition Lazarus was in to his wickedness; and hastily conclude,

clude, that he had brought himself into such circumstances, and was suffering no more than he deserved. Presumptuous, uncharitable, and cruel as the supposition was, yet he might take it for granted without the least examination; and make use of it to justify or excuse to himself his neglect of him.——Hence we may see the probability of the description, and its consistency, propriety, and pertinence to the occasion. For to palliate their inhumanity with a pretext of piety, was the true pharisaic spirit. The more uncommon and terrible the calamity, the more were these men disposed to consider it as *a judgment of God*, and to infer from it the greater guilt of the sufferers, instead of their own greater obligation to assist and relieve them. In like manner they were apt to look upon prosperity, as a proof, not only of worldly prudence, but of real worth and divine favor: tho' they might easily have learned better sentiments from their own scriptures, especially from the book of *Job*; which is admirably

admirably calculated to shew, that misfortunes are not in themselves any sign of guilt, or prosperity of innocence.——If we duly consider, then, this prevailing notion and temper of that party; we may perceive not only the design, but the force and beauty of this part of the parable, as addressed to them. We have included in our narration the rich man's character, for the sake of explanation. But our Savior thought fit to avoid all mention of the character either of the rich or the poor man: probably, not only for the sake of delicacy, but in order to point out with greater clearness and strength, the injustice and absurdity of concluding, from any circumstances that may befal men in this world, what is their real character and estimation in the judgment of God. For no sooner did the two persons, whose respective conditions in this world, in which they lived and died, are so thorowly marked, appear in the other world, than behold a total reverse. In that state indeed, though not in this, characters may be inferred from circumstances. And therefore, our Savior leaves it, with a perfect propriety, to his audience to make the inference; and in their own minds to add to his edition of the story, that the rich man utterly despised and neglected the other, and suffered him to perish miserably, without the least pity; and therefore, was justly punished for his inhumanity, by being reduced to the like distress, and to beg for the smallest charity at the hand of *Lazarus* in vain.

If we observe the contrasts, between the poor man's lying at the gate abandoned by human society, and surrounded by the dogs, and his being conducted by the angels to the bosom of his ancestor *Abraham*——the rich man's being cloathed with purple and fine linen, and faring sumptuously every day; and his being encompassed with flames and enduring intense and unquenchable thirst—the patient silence of the one, and the importunate cry of the other——

the crumb of bread, and *the drop of water*; nothing can be conceived more exquisitely wrought.——The term tranflated, beggar, would be more properly rendered, the poor man. For the expreffion concerning him, is not intreating or begging, but only *defiring* to be fed with the crumbs which fell from the rich man's table.

It is worthy of our obfervation, that the patriarch not only vouchfafes an anfwer to the fuppliant criminal; but even in alleging the juftice of the cafe, ufes the fofteft expreffions imaginable, gives him the title of *fon* in return for the appellation of *father*, and couches all his reproof under the word *remember*. Nay, as if he felt the ftrongeft difpofition to grant him fome relief, he feems to recollect himfelf, as it were, and plead the impoffibility of it.

There is not the leaft intimation given in the text as to the duration of the condemned criminal's mifery. Only we may argue

argue from analogy, that as *Lazarus* was suffered to perish in misery by his inhumanity; so he was left to be utterly consumed in that *unquenchable fire*, which would sooner or later put an end to his *other life*, and with it his *being for ever*.

THE world to come is the object, not of our sight or experience, but of our faith. And the rewards and punishments of it are so imperfectly understood as to afford room for little certainty, but much conjecture, and consequently much error. For where our knowledge is the least, imagination often takes the place of reason, and is most busy and extravagant. Hence some *Christian* writers, in describing future rewards and punishments, have given a licentious and unwarrantable scope to their own fancy: and particularly, in the latter instance have delivered rather the suggestions of a dark and savage imagination, than the dictates of sober reason, or the tenſe of holy Scripture——describing condemned

demned criminals in the other world as filled with inextinguishable rage against the Almighty, and wishing with infatiable fury to involve others in the same punishment, and to aggravate their miseries.——These may be *Mahometan* sentiments, but certainly not *Christian*. *Mahomet* put this sentence into the mouth of the damned; *Lord, increase the torments of them that have seduced us.* But our *Savior* represents the criminal in a state of punishment, not as arraigning the divine justice, but as supplicating, in the most humble as well as earnest expressions, the least mitigation of his torment, as an act of pure mercy and compassion, and making use of no other plea to obtain it, than the greatness of his misery: and when he was convinced, that it could not be granted him, as acknowledging, by his silence in his own behalf, the justice of his punishment; and then preferring, with the like earnestness, another petition for his five brethren on earth, left they also should come into that place of torment.——
This

This account is perfectly reasonable and natural. As it is usual for condemned criminals in this world to acknowledge the justice of their sentence, and to warn others, lest by the like criminal practices they should come to the like miserable end; so we may conclude, both from reason and from our Savior's authority, that in the other world, the suffering criminals are more sensible of their own guilt, and of the perfect justice and goodness of the Deity, than to blaspheme him with accusations of tyranny; and that they conceive a horror at the thoughts of others being involved in the like guilt and misery, especially their relatives or friends remaining on earth.—— Let us then attend to our Savior's own account, and give no credit to the crude suggestions of presumptuous men.

The favor which the suffering criminal so earnestly implored for his five brethren, was no less than the dispatch of a messenger from the other world, to make a miraculous

lous appearance, for no other end, than their particular conviction and reformation: as apprehending that other means were not sufficient, but that this would be effectual. The patriarch intimates in his answer, that they had already what they themselves owned to be a revelation from heaven. *They have Moses and the prophets, let them hear them.* These were the great reformers of religion and teachers of morality to the *Jewish* nation, whose wisdom, integrity, and authority they expresly acknowledged. If then they would pay no attention to the instructions and persuasions of persons who were confessedly of so high a character; must *Lazarus* be sent from the dead to reform them? Could he come with greater authority than that which they attributed to the prophets? Could he deliver better instructions and more powerful admonitions? or if he could, were they worthy of such favor? Is men's resisting a present evidence, though confessedly sufficient, or their abusing present advantages,

though

though superior to what others enjoy, a reason why still greater should be afforded them? If they are not influenced by the dictates of reason, conscience, and humanity, enforced by written laws and instructions, which themselves own to bear the highest authority; must a special and singular revelation be made to them for their conviction alone, and to overcome their wilful negligence and perverseness? Is this a reasonable demand?

No reply could be made to these questions, with any appearance of reason, but that which our Savior puts into the mouth of the supplicant. *Nay, Father Abraham, but if one went unto them from the dead, they will repent.*——Here he plainly reduces all he could urge in support of his petition to one point, an appeal to the event; alledging that this method would certainly be effectual. To which the patriarch replies, by denying the supposed consequence. *If,* saith he, *they hear not Moses and the prophets;*
neither

neither will they be perfuaded, though one arofe from the dead.

LET us confider the meaning and truth of this affertion.——It cannot be inferred merely from men's refifting a lefs evidence of truth or motive to virtue, that they will therefore refift a greater. This is not a juft inference in itfelf, nor at all implied or fuppofed in the text: but only, that bad men may arrive to fuch an inveterate prejudice and malignity as to be unconvinceable by the cleareft evidence, and incorrigible by the moft extraordinary means: and that they are actually arrived to this hardened ftate of mind, whenever prefent fufficient evidences and motives have no effect upon them.——This fentiment we fhall find agreeable to experience. And thus, the fenfe of the *patriarch* perfectly coincides with the intention of our *Savior*, to predict, from the prefent malignity of temper in the *pharifees* and *fcribes*, that they would not be converted even by his own

own resurrection from the dead.—Wheresoever less arguments and motives produce some good effect; there it may be presumed that greater will produce more: but if they have no effect at all; the contrary inference may be made. The reason is, because this implies so thorow a dishonesty, as is proof against all conviction. It is indeed to be hoped, that as there are but few men in the world of a perfect integrity, there are as few of this opposite character. But nevertheless, in any affair whatsoever, if men are previously determined to give no attention to, or not to be guided by, the evidence of things; it makes no difference, whether the evidence be smaller or greater: as he who shuts his eyes will not distinguish objects the better by any encrease of light.—Instances of this kind are so far from being singular and unaccountable, that they have occured but too frequently. It hath been often observed in common disputations, that where a strong prejudice has once been raised, no arguments would afterward convince.

convince. Even in courts of juftice, where the ftricteft attention is due to evidence, it hath been fometimes known, that the court has been previoufly refolved to pay no regard at all to the merits of the caufe: In which cafe it is plain, that no addition of evidence would anfwer any purpofe.— In matters of *doctrine*, if men have once fet afide all evidence of reafon concerning the fubject, there is no poffibility of convincing them of their error, even by the cleareft arguments.——And in regard to *practice*, it is certain from experience, that the weightieft *motives* do not always determine men to action, any more than the ftrongeft *reafons* convince their underftandings. It is often found that the moft trivial and uncertain confiderations have a greater effect than arguments of the higheft probability and motives of infinite moment.—In fhort, conviction and reformation do not depend fo much upon the degree of evidence or weight of motives which are offered, as upon men's difpofition sition or aversion to receive that evidence, and feel that weight; and passion, prejudice, interest, appetite, or vanity, are often sufficient singly, much more in conjunction, to inspire a hatred of the opposite truth; and that hatred, when strengthened by habit, will be unconquerable by any proof whatsoever.—To apply these remarks to religion and divine revelation.— They who attend to, and honestly improve the means and motives afforded them at present, would make (it may be fairly presumed) a like good use of greater. An honest *heathen*, who is attentive to the light of nature and the dictates of his own conscience, would also have been observant, if educated a *Jew*, of the moral instructions of *Moses* and the *prophets*. And if the same person had afterward been present at the discourses and miracles of our *Savior*, he would have become a sincere believer in him. And such a *Christian*, being fully persuaded of *Christ*'s resurrection, would have no need that a messenger should be

sent

fent to him from the dead; nor would fuch an appearance be in reality of any ufe or benefit to him.—On the other hand, if we fuppofe a *heathen* fo wicked, as not to be at all influenced by the law written in his own heart, or the dictates of his own confcience; neither would he have paid any regard, if he had been a *Jew*, to the law of *Mofes*, or the inftructions of the *prophets*. If a *Jew* gave no attention to *Mofes* and the *prophets*, neither would he believe in our *Savior* or his *apoftles*. And it may be affirmed in like manner, that if the admonitions of *Chrift* and his *apoftles* have no effect upon a *Chriftian*, neither will he be perfuaded tho' one arofe from the dead.—It may be imagined by inconfiderate perfons, that the amazing appearance and awful meffage of a perfon from the dead, would make fo deep an impreffion, as could neither be worn out by time, nor effaced by the returning power of vicious habits. But this fuppofition is contrary to experience. For there have not been wanting examples of wicked perfons, who have firmly believed, that they both faw and heard an apparition from the dead exhorting them to repent; and confequently have been thorowly alarmed for a while; yet, foon after, have returned to their former vices. And though the apparition was the mere working of a difturbed imagination; it would have the fame effect as if it had been real, fo long as they believed it. We might add here the fimilar examples of wicked perfons, who have been ftruck with the fear of approaching death, and with the utmoft earneftnefs have refolved to repent, if God would pleafe in his great mercy to fpare their lives: yet have no fooner recovered their former health, than their vices have regained their former ftrength and afcendancy. Such inftances are fufficient to prove, that the greateft aftonifhment or terror of the imagination, if not fupported by rational conviction, deliberate attention, and fteady refolution, will in time vanifh away,

away, and give place to opposite prejudices and passions. In all such cases, the habitual temper of the mind is like a spring held down only by a superior weight: it makes a continual resistance, and in proportion as the weight is taken off, returns to its former position.—It cannot be difficult, then, for any person, who has a proper knowledge of human nature, to conceive, how certainly it may be inferred, from men's neglect of the means, and resistance of the motives, offered them at present, to repentance and virtue, that even the most extraordinary and alarming methods would not prevail. Since such neglect and resistance necessarily imply, that their vicious habits are already so fixed, and their minds so hardened, as to be incapable of a real and lasting change. And therefore, even the miraculous appearance of a person from the dead to admonish them, would only produce a transient consternation, without any permanent effect in an amendment of life.

Now, from a general review of the parable, we may take occasion to contemplate the justice of divine providence in this and a future state, as connected together.—— There are abundant marks of divine justice observable in this life. But it operates more internally than externally; and the effects of it are felt more than seen. Hence the remorse, shame, fear, and forebodings of a guilty mind: and hence the homefelt peace and satisfaction of the honest and generous heart. There is indeed in some instances a visible distribution of rewards and punishments. For human government is a divine ordinance, for the punishment of evil doers, and the security of them that do well. Hence, the guilty are often punished, and the worthy rewarded by human society. But the provision of divine justice in the frame of the mind itself, by which every person becomes his own rewarder or punisher is more extensive. Yet this takes place only in a certain degree, proper to the imperfect reason, social nature,

nature, and probationary ftate of mankind. On this foundation we may build a moral proof of rewards and punifhments in a future ftate. As the general conftitution of human nature fhews a plan of divine juftice begun and continually proceeding, but not finifhed or made compleat, in this life; therefore, we may affuredly expect another life, in which it will proceed to greater perfection. Great inequalities often prefent themfelves to our obfervation in this world. Some of them are indeed only or chiefly in appearance: but others, it muft be confeffed, are real. Sometimes the wicked man profpers, enjoys power and pleafure, lives long in health and wealth, and dies without a pang: whilft another, of real worth and goodnefs, is worn out with poverty and mifery. Let us not be ftartled at fuch events, and tempted to diftruft the juftice of the Deity: but always remember, that the fcheme of infinite wifdom is not to be meafured by the narrow compafs of this world; but is
higher

higher than heaven, deeper than hell, longer than the earth, and broader than the sea——That it comprehends all ages, states, and worlds, in one unbounded and everlasting series. If then he does not see fit to rectify things in the time or manner our weak fancy may suggest, as most necessary or expedient, shall we therefore presume to doubt of his justice?——the *Psalmist* experienced this kind of temptation, when he tells us, *That his feet were almost gone, his steps had well nigh slipt: for he was envious at the foolish man, when he saw the prosperity of the wicked: till he went into the sanctuary of* G O D, *and there learned to know their end.* Surely, says he, *thou didst set them in slippery places, thou castedst them down into destruction. How are they brought into desolation in a moment, they are utterly consumed with terrors!*

In Hades, or the invisible state, saith our Savior, *he lift up his eyes, being in torments.*—— Will the infidel reject this as mere fable, void

void of all real foundation in the nature of things?——Are there no real miseries endured in this world?——Have there not been examples even of good men perishing in lingering torments, by the oppression and malice of cruel persecutors? and shall those wicked oppressors themselves escape? Shall they not feel, in their turn, the miseries they have inflicted upon the innocent? Shall they abuse the power they were entrusted with to so diabolical a purpose, yet have nothing to dread from the power of almighty God? Shall death be their security, and the grave a sure refuge from the scourge of eternal justice? Or shall persevering innocence and virtue be exposed to the neglect of selfish, and the violence of tyrannical men, and never find protection or redress from the righteous governor of the world?——Reason remonstrates against it, and our *Christian* faith confirms the contrary truth.

Of all the criminal actions men commit, those which are most inhuman are certainly

certainly moſt obnoxious to divine juſtice, and will be puniſhed in the moſt exemplary manner. For it is a juſt ſentence, *They ſhall have judgment without mercy, who have ſhewed no mercy.*

Nothing can be conceived more proper than the repreſentation in this parable, to warn perſons in affluent circumſtances, from ſuffering their hearts to be corrupted and hardened by the deceitfulneſs of riches, or the allurements of luxury; ſo as to become wholly ſelfiſh and inſenſible of the wants and miſeries of others. The figure deſcribed of the wealthy man, in another world,—in the midſt of torments,—paſſionately begging,—for *a drop of water,*—from the hand of *that very perſon,*—to whom, when periſhing by want, he had denied *the crumbs of his table,*—points out to us both the guilt and the puniſhment of inhumanity in too ſtriking a view not to leave a deep impreſſion upon every attentive and ingenuous mind.——Let us be

perſuaded

persuaded by it to abhor all cruelty, as we would avoid our own misery; and to preserve and cherish the dispositions of kindness, compassion, and liberality. As we hope for the mercy of GOD in the day of judgment, let us compassionate the sufferings of our fellow-creatures, and be ready to relieve them. *Blessed are the merciful, for they shall obtain mercy.*

"BUT am I responsible," says the uncharitable man, "for the condition of others?—Should not every one learn in the first place to take care of himself, and, if he is unfortunate, to bear with patience his own burden?—There is no end of supplying other men's wants—must I impoverish myself to save others from poverty?—what is *Lazarus* to me?—I did not bring him into those circumstances, and therefore am not obliged to deliver him from them—I do him no injury, and leave him to his fate."——Such are the sentiments of the

the selfish man; though he may not think fit to express them, for fear of the resentments of human society. But the answer to such language, as far as it can be thought to have any color of reason, is obvious. GOD hath made a proper and liberal provision for the wants of his creatures in general; and will indeed deliver his suffering servants in due time from every evil. But in the present state, he hath connected mankind together in society; that they might become his willing instruments in assisting and relieving one another. This wise and gracious design of heaven in the constitution of our nature, appears as evidently as the sun in its greatest lustre. He then that is void of charity and compassion, hath corrupted and violated his own nature; and sets his selfish and inhuman temper in the most direct opposition to the benignity and goodness, the will and design of the all-wise Maker and Governor of the world; and consequently exposes himself to the most dreadful effects of his power and justice.

THE

The sentiments of our blessed Savior on this subject may be sufficiently collected from the foregoing parable: to which we may add another passage, too memorable to be ever forgot, in his description of his own administration of the final judgment: which shews how much acts of mercy and goodness, or instances of selfishness and inhumanity, will be the ground of men's eternal salvation or condemnation. Matth. xxv. 34. *Then shall the King say unto them on his right hand, Come ye blessed of my Father, inherit the kingdom prepared for you from the foundation of the world. For I was an hungred, and ye gave me meat: I was thirsty, and ye gave me drink: I was a stranger, and ye took me in: Naked, and ye clothed me: I was sick, and ye visited me: I was in prison, and ye came unto me. Then shall the righteous answer him, saying, Lord, when saw we thee an hungred, and fed thee? or thirsty, and gave thee drink? When saw we thee a stranger, and took thee in? or naked, and clothed thee? Or when saw we thee*

thee sick, or in prison, and came unto thee? And the King shall answer, and say unto them, Verily I say unto you, In as much as ye have done it unto one of the least of these my brethren, ye have done it unto me. Then shall he say also unto them on the left hand, Depart from me, ye cursed, into everlasting fire, prepared for the devil and his angels. For I was an hungred, and ye gave me no meat: I was thirsty, and ye gave me no drink: I was a stranger, and ye took me not in: Naked, and ye clothed me not: Sick, and in prison, and ye visited me not. Then shall they also answer him, saying, Lord, when saw we thee an hungred, or athirst, or a stranger, or naked, or sick, or in prison, and did not minister unto thee? Then shall he answer them, saying, Verily I say unto you, In as much as ye did it not to one of the least of these, ye did it not to me. And these shall go away into everlasting punishment: but the righteous into life eternal.

DISCOURSE IX.

Our Savior reproves the Vanity of his Apostles.

Luke xvii. 1—10.

Then said he unto the disciples, It is impossible but that offences will come: but wo unto him through whom they come. It were better for him that a milstone were hanged about his neck, and he cast into the sea, than that he should offend one of these little ones. Take heed to yourselves: If thy brother trespass against thee, rebuke him; and if he repent, forgive him. And if he trespass against thee seven times in a day, and seven times in a day turn again to thee, saying, I repent; thou shalt forgive him. And the apostles said unto the Lord, Increase our faith. And the Lord said, If ye had faith as a grain of mustard-seed, ye might say unto this sycamine-tree, Be thou plucked up by the root, and be thou planted in the sea;

sea; and it should obey you. But which of you having a servant plowing, or feeding cattle, will say unto him by and by, when he is come from the field, Go and sit down to meat? And will not rather say unto him, Make ready wherewith I may sup, and gird thyself, and serve me, till I have eaten and drunken; and afterward thou shalt eat and drink? Doth he thank that servant because he did the things that were commanded him? I trow not. So likewise ye, when ye shall have done all those things which are commanded you, say, We are unprofitable servants: we have done that which was our duty to do.

THE first verses of the text plainly appear to have a reference to the foregoing contest between our Savior and the pharisees and scribes, and the endeavors they had used to destroy his reputation, and to alienate the hearts of the people from him: and they contain a denunciation of wo for their wicked attempts

to

to frustrate his benevolent purpose of reclaiming the publicans and sinners, and of establishing his disciples in their faith and obedience. He begins with laying down this observation, *It is impossible*, or, it is not to be expected, *but that offences will come: i. e.* Considering the state of the world, his doctrine would certainly meet with opposition, and raise enmity in the minds of such men as the pharisees and scribes: And considering their character and disposition, they would undoubtedly proceed, as they had begun, to give him all the offence in their power, lay every stumbling-block in his way, and raise all possible obstruction to the progress he was making, in converting and reforming the people. But there was so much injustice and malice in such attempts, that he affirms with the utmost solemnity, That whosoever was guilty of prejudicing the mind, even of the meanest persons there present, (for whom he had a kind regard, implied by the term of affection, *little-ones*) against his inftructions, and thereby feducing them from becoming his difciples, it would have been better for that man to have fuffered the moft violent and untimely death, than to have committed fo criminal an offence. From which it appears, that he did not mean by the term, *offence*, fuch little perfonal flights and provocations, as frequently occur in the world, and which are often repaid with a refentment, if not entirely groundlefs, yet difproportionate to the nature of them. But he means that crafty induftrious defigned malevolent oppofition to his influence and the fuccefs of the gofpel which he taught, as implied a high degree of guilt. The pharifees and fcribes pretended to find matter in our Savior's inftructions and manner of life, and efpecially, in the humanity and tendernefs he difcovered for the publicans and finners, not only of juft objection to him, but of high contempt of him, and refentment againft him. They conftrued his behavior into an offence againft themfelves:

selves: But in fact, they were the aggreſ-
fors, the malicious injurious offending
party; and he had never injured, nor in
reaſon offended them: unleſs the nobleſt
exertions of wiſdom and virtue, were to
be deemed an offence. And indeed to
perſons of very bad diſpoſitions, the higheſt
inſtance of goodneſs may poſſibly in ſome
caſes be the higheſt provocation, and ſerve
only to enflame their rage, and give a
keener edge to their malicious intentions.
From the beginning of his public mini-
ſtration, they began to cenſure his conduct,
object to his doctrine, and calumniate his
character: and no vindications of his own
conduct would ſatisfy them, no expoſtu-
lations or arguments convince them, no
admonitions reclaim them, though conveyed under parabolic images the moſt
ſenſible and affecting that can be conceived.
On the contrary, all his repreſentations
rather ſerved in effect to increaſe their averſion, and exaſperate their malice. For
ſpiritual as well as bodily remedies, even

the beft and nobleft that can be applied, if they fail of curing or aſſwaging the diftemper, will probably operate to a contrary purpoſe, and ferve to provoke and heighten it. If they were not fatisfied with our LORD's vindication of his own conduct, in the beautiful parables of the careful fhepherd and the good father; if they treated him with infolence and difdain on account of his parable of the unjuft fteward, and the following admonitions againft covetoufnefs and an abufe of wealth; it is hardly to be fuppoſed, that even the noble and ftriking reprefentation of the rich man and Lazarus, would be effectual to their conviction and reformation: but they would, notwithſtanding, perfift in their malicious purpoſes and endeavors, to blaft his character, deſtroy his influence, and prevent him from gaining converts among the people. Therefore, when he had finifhed the foregoing parable, in which he had predicted, by the mouth of their anceftor Abraham, their final unbelief and impenitence,

impenitence, he immediately turns about to his own difciples, and with a view to confirm them in their faith and allegiance, fays to them, *It is impoffible*, or, it is not to be expected, *but that offences will come: but wo unto him through whom they come. It were better for him that a milftone were hanged about his neck, and he caft into the fea, than that he fhould offend one of thefe little ones.*

He then takes occafion, from the late conteft, to inftruct them as to their behavior. For the infolence and malice which the pharifees and fcribes difcovered againft him would naturally tend to raife *their* indignation, in proportion to the efteem and affection they conceived for him. He therefore charges them to take heed to themfelves, and to beware of entertaining a groundlefs animofity or implacable refentment againft any one. And in cafe of their receiving any real injury or abufe; firft to rebuke the offending party: and if he difcovered marks of repentance; then, though

though the injury or offence was ever so great, to forgive him: and though the trespass should be repeated ever so often, even seven times in a day, still, sincere repentance should always be accepted; tho' without repentance there is no ground of forgiveness.

THEN the apostles said unto him, *Lord, increase our faith.*—This seems to refer to the scorn and aversion with which they perceived the pharisees and scribes to treat our Savior. It is not to be wondered, if the opposition of such considerable persons, made an impression upon the minds, even of those who had the strongest faith in him. The apostles therefore, being fully satisfied with his vindication of himself, and charmed with the wisdom, propriety, and beauty of his parables, thought fit, at this juncture, to signify their firm adherence to him, notwithstanding any attempts to over-awe, corrupt, or seduce them: but at the same time they were

desirous

desirous that he would *increase their faith*, by adding to the wisdom of his instructions some *new proofs* of his *power* and authority: and probably it was their secret wish, that he would, then and there, work some stupenduous miracle, as an occasion of triumph to them, and of confusion to his and their enemies. However, they seemed to make a great merit, at this time, of their belief in him and adherence to him, considering the discouragements and temptations they met with. Upon which, he assures them, that how much soever they might plume themselves upon the greatness and strength of their faith in him, they had in reality, as yet, but a very poor stock of it. For if they had a real faith and confidence in him, though in the smallest proportion to the excellence of those instructions they had heard from him, and the power of those mighty works they had seen him perform; all objections would vanish: the greatest opposition and discouragements he or they could possibly meet with, would not make the leaft impreffion upon them: the mountains of difficulty, which they imagined to lie in their way, would appear lefs than mole-hills: and inftead of being weakly intimidated or feduced from following him, and ftaggered in their faith in his miracles, they would themfelves become able to work the greateft miracles;—to command, for inftance, if occafion were, this fycamine-tree (pointing to one that ftood by) to be rooted up, and planted in the fea; and it would obey them.

The apoftles themfelves at firft followed our Savior with a ftrong expectation, that he would rife to be a great prince, and beftow worldly rewards and preferments upon his friends and favorites. Hence they frequently ftrove one with another who fhould be the foremoft in his favor; and fought to advance themfelves in his opinion, by fhewing their great affection to his perfon, their firm adherence to his caufe, and their zeal in his fervice; which they

they were fometimes tempted to boaft of in his prefence. We find a fpecimen of this fpirit in the apoftle Peter, on a particular occafion. For when our Savior had told the young gentleman who was poffeffed of great wealth, that if he would be perfect in virtue, he muft give up all his poffeffions and follow him, and then he fhould have abundant treafures in heaven; *Lo*, faith Peter upon that occafion, *we have left all, and followed thee: what fhall we have therefore?*—From which it appears, he thought there was no fmall fhare of merit in fuch conduct: though in fact, the worldly All he had relinquifhed to follow CHRIST, amounted to but a fmall value: however, it was his all, and he was willing to make the moft of it, and feemed to think himfelf entitled to fome confiderable honor and reward from our SAVIOR.

IT was very natural then for the apoftles, upon the occafion of the foregoing parables, when

when they saw him confronted and insulted by men of such rank and character, as many of the scribes and pharisees were, to assume to themselves the more merit from their steady attachment to him, in proportion to the contempt and opposition he met with from others : though, perhaps, they did not openly avow the high opinion they conceived of themselves on that account. But as our Savior knew the hearts of men, and it was his constant manner to speak directly to the very inmost thoughts and sentiments of his hearers, and frequently even before they had an opportunity of expressing them ; so here, it may be supposed, he perceived this vain and self-assuming spirit arising in the minds of his disciples : and therefore addressed himself to them in the following familiar expostulation :—" If any of you had a servant,
" who had finished his labor in the field,
" would you not expect as is customary,
" that he should be ready to pay his per-
" sonal attendance upon you ? And would
" you

" you think that he conferred an obliga-
" tion upon you by such attendance? And
" that you were bound to gratify him
" with some extraordinary reward, for
" his discharging the customary duty of
" a servant? I suppose not—Learn then
" not to presume because of your atten-
" dance on me, who am your master.
" Though you may listen to my instruc-
" tions, and obey my commands, though
" you may follow me from one place to
" another, and do me many personal ser-
" vices, nay though you may bear with
" some abuse, and undergo some difficul-
" ties and hardships on that account; yet
" know and consider that all this is no
" more than your duty: beware of assum-
" ing merit to yourselves: your attendance
" on me is not for my profit and emolu-
" ment, but your own: respect, gratitude,
" and thanks are due, not from me to
" you, but from you to me, from the ser-
" vant to his master. When you have
" done all in your power to serve me and
                                    " advance

"advance my honor in the world, the
"language moſt becoming you is this, We
"are but unprofitable ſervants—we have
"only done that which was our duty. So
"that whatever honor or reward you
"may expect or receive from me, it will
"be the effect of my favor and liberality,
"rather than of your deſert."——Thus he
repreſſed the ſpirit of pride and preſumption, which he ſaw ariſing in the minds of his diſciples, and leads them to a proper knowledge of their own ſituation and character, as his ſervants.

HERE ends the memorable converſation, which paſſed between our Savior and his numerous audience, conſiſting of publicans and ſinners, of ſcribes and phariſees, and of his own diſciples.

Now in taking a ſummary view of the whole, we cannot avoid obſerving the inimitable ſimplicity of manner, variety of invention, and propriety of figures, by

which

which he vindicates his own conduct, and shews the paternal goodness of his own disposition; exhibits the dissolute and disgraceful character of the publicans and sinners, and encourages them to repentance; exposes the incorrigible pride and malignity of the pharisees and scribes; and finally remarks the temper of his own disciples, and applies to them pertinent instructions and admonitions. In all which we may discern admirable marks of his wisdom, integrity, and benevolence. He perfectly understood both how to defend himself, and attack his opponents—was thorowly disposed to do good to all men—but was so far from courting either the favor of the great, or the affections of the populace, by any kind of adulation or artifice; that he reprehended the prejudices and vices, the vanity and folly, of every part of his audience, not excepting his own disciples. And we have reason to believe, that his instructions produced a happy effect both upon them, and upon many of the publicans and sinners. But in regard to the pharisees and scribes, the contrary. For what signs will move the obdurate to repent? what arguments will convince, what eloquence persuade, men who have no faith, no sincerity, no honesty of heart? men whose minds are swollen with pride, made callous by covetousness, and hardened by hypocrisy?——They could not easily avoid applying the characters of the unjust steward, of the inhuman rich man and of his five brethren, who paid no regard to Moses and the prophets, and concerning whom Abraham predicts, that neither would they be persuaded, though one arose from the dead—they could not avoid applying these characters to themselves, and feeling the smart of these strokes in their own consciences. They were then, as we may suppose, cut to the heart; and probably went away full of resentment, and with purposes of deadly hatred and revenge. For in all contentions the unjust and injurious party are most averse to reconciliation,

liation, and feldom forgive thofe they have injured. And the certain effect of admonition and reproof, where it does not ferve to convince and reclaim, is to provoke. Accordingly we find, in the courfe of the gofpel-hiftory, that the fame fort of men, the pharifees and priefts, who had all along infulted our Savior in perfon, calumniated his character, and endeavored to deftroy his influence, at laft confpired alfo againft his life,—bribed *Judas* to betray him,—caufed him to be apprehended as if he had been a thief,—fuborned witneffes againft him,—inftigated the populace, to demand the releafe of *Barabbas*, who was a robber, in preference to him,—and to clamor aloud, Crucify him, crucify him— threatened the governor *Pilate*, if he would not deliver him into their power——proceeded with infatiable malice to infult him when dying upon the crofs—and hired the Roman foldiers to fay, when he was rifen from the dead, that his difciples came by night whilft they were afleep and ftole him away!——

away!——So true was the prophetic declaration concerning them, that neither would they be perfuaded, though one arofe from the dead!

Having thus confidered at large the conduct of our Savior's enemies, the pharifees, and fhewn the motives upon which they acted, and to what excefs of wickednefs their enmity againft him tranfported them;——Let us beware of being guilty, in any meafure, of the like offences. Whofoever, through malice and hypocrify, or with interefted and ambitious views, infufes prejudices into the minds of others againft true religion——feduces, or compels them to act againft their own confcience——lays temptations and fnares in their way, to corrupt their judgment, or alienate their hearts from truth and virtue——or applies human doctrines, or authority, or example, or any motives of this world, in oppofition to the authority of our Savior and the influence of his gofpel;——he is guilty, in proportion

portion, of the offence denoted by our Savior in the text, and renders himself subject to the wo denounced against *him by whom such offence cometh.*

Let us learn also to take heed to ourselves, and to consider well, with what temper of mind we hear the instructions and admonitions of our Savior. For the consequence of our frequently reading or hearing them will be, that we shall either become more improved in virtue, or more hardened in iniquity and deceit. There is a certain docility and candor of mind in some persons, which renders them apt to receive benefit from the gospel, to grow wiser by instruction, and better by reproof: they are willing to understand, acknowledge, and amend their errors and failings. The disciples of our Savior, and many of the publicans and sinners, were of this happy disposition. But there are persons in the world of a contrary temper; and who, like the pharisees and scribes, are too conceited

conceited to be taught, too proud to be admonifhed, too obftinate to be perfuaded, too wicked to be amended, by any methods that human or divine wifdom fhall fee fit to be ufed.——Let us then examine ourfelves;—how far we are of a docile perfuadable and amicable fpirit; or of the contrary difpofition, violent, arrogant, imperfuadable, unconvinceable, abounding in our own fenfe, and full of our own merit. Let us confider, that it is the property of the wife man to hear inftruction and to increafe in learning, and of the honeft man to improve in goodnefs: but of fools to hate knowledge and inftruction.

FINALLY, Let us always remember, that were our conduct ever fo unblameable, and our minds ever fo free from error and prejudice; had we done all the things which are commanded us, filled up our refpective ftations in life with the utmoft fidelity and diligence, and exhaufted all our abilities in ufeful fervices to mankind; yet,

yet, in respect to our common Lord and Master, we should be but unprofitable servants, and have done no more than was our duty. How much more then should a consciousness of the many imperfections which adhere to us, damp the spirit of vanity and insolence, and lead us to humility and penitence?

Now that we may all be sincerely and cordially disposed to hear, understand, reflect upon, and apply, in the whole conduct of life, those instructions of our Savior, which are fit to convince us of our errors and offences, and to make us *wise unto salvation*, God grant of his infinite mercy by Jesus Christ our Lord.

APPENDIX.

THE authors of the Monthly Review (to whose critical judgment some respect is unquestionably due) have recommended to my attention the remarks which the Reverend Mr. *Mason* has made upon the two volumes of discourses I have before published. I shall therefore here give an answer to these remarks: as it may serve to explain my own meaning in the passages quoted; and may perhaps contribute to the satisfaction of the many friends, who have not only favored me with their subscriptions to the edition, but honored me with their approbation of the contents of those volumes.

In regard to the propriety and justice of Mr. *Mason*'s remarks, those will judge, who think it worth their while to examine them and my answer.—The charges he brings against me are, that I contradict the New Testament, and myself—two very material charges: one affecting me as an author, and the other as a *Christian.*

In answer to which, let me premise in general, that many authors of superior ability and reputation have been accused of contradicting themselves, when the inconsistency has lain entirely in the misconception of the reader: and that it is almost impossible for any man to write with sense and freedom upon subjects of divinity, without being accused by some party or other, of denying some real or supposed doctrine of Christianity.

To come now to the instances which Mr. *Mason* gives of my contradicting myself.——In my advertisement to the reader, I have

I have said, "That the writers of the New Testament always mean by the term Αναςασες or *resurrection*, a restoration to life; or that operation or event, by which the person who dies passes from death to life." I have also said afterwards, Vol. I. p. 274. "That the term *resurrection* in Scripture always means a future state." This appears to Mr. *Mason*'s understanding to be a gross contradiction, and he represents it as such—because the passage to a future state, and the state itself, are different.—But if Mr. *Mason* will recollect himself, I cannot but think he will easily perceive, that one idea includes the other. For if there be a future state, there must be a resurrection or passage to that state: and *vice versa*, a resurrection to another life or future state includes that future state. If so, all he can charge upon me is an inaccuracy of expression, arising from the addition of the word *always*. And this seeming inaccuracy will vanish, if both passages be compared together,

together, and understood as they were meant, *viz.* that the term *resurrection* in Scripture signifies a transition to another state or life; and consequently implies that state or life, "*always without any reference to what becomes of the body.*" See Advert. Part 1st.

Again, I say, vol. 1. p. 351. "That in reality, a general reformation of mankind in any high degree, seems to be impracticable by any means whatsoever:" and yet in a few pages after, (p. 362.) I say, "We have indeed ground to hope, that the gospel will have in some future ages more extensive and beneficial effects, than it has hitherto obtained: because the same spirit of prophecy which predicted, in so strong and remarkable terms, the infatuation, corruption, and slavery of the *Christian* nations, hath foretold also as clearly their deliverance and reformation—a reformation which hath already taken place

"in a confiderable degree in fome nations,
"as we have the happinefs to experience:
"and all wife *Chriftians* are waiting the
"conduct of providence in order to the
"accomplifhment of the whole, in a uni-
"verfal change of the *Chriftian* world, and
"the converfion of the *Jews* and other
"nations. And this will be, in a religious
"fenfe, the kingdom and glory of our Sa-
"vior on earth."——The reflection Mr.
Mafon makes is this, "Sure then, the re-
"formation of mankind in a high degree
"is not impracticable by any means what-
"foever."

But nothing can be more eafy than to reconcile thefe two paffages:—For, *in a high degree* is a comparative expreffion. Thefe nations are already reformed, *in a high degree*, compared to the ignorance, idolatry, and corruption of former times. And if ever this change fhould become univerfal, and the *Jews* and other nations be converted to Chriftianity; there will

be

be a reformation of mankind *in a far higher degree* than any that hath already taken place. Yet it may be true, nevertheless, that a general reformation of mankind *in any high degree* may be impracticable by any means whatsoever, *compared* to the perfection of a future state. And I am persuaded Mr. *Mason* will readily agree with me in this opinion. And that this is my meaning, the whole paragraph, and the whole discourse, shews so evidently, that I wonder it should escape the remarker's observation. For the whole paragraph is this, (p. 351.) " In reality, a
" general reformation of mankind in any
" high degree, seems to be impracticable
" by any means whatsoever: the consti-
" tution of this world does not seem to
" admit of it. Human nature will still
" remain the same, and mankind are and
" always will be creatures beset with temp-
" tations, appetites, passions, errors, fol-
" lies, and faults. This world is not a
" state in which the virtue, peace, and
" happiness

"happiness of mankind can ever be tho-
"rowly established. So great a change,
"so happy a reformation, so divine an
"establishment, cannot take place but in
"that state or world where our blessed
"*Savior's* kingdom is established, that
"everlasting kingdom of his, into which
"all sincere and good men shall be finally
"admitted, and form one glorious society
"under his protection and government."
This is far from asserting, that mankind
may not be reformed in this world much
more than they are at present.

He thinks, I contradict the tenor of the
New Testament, in saying, vol. 1. p. 352.
"That the reformation of mankind in
"this world, is not represented in the
"writings of the New Testament, as be-
"ing the principal end and design of our
"*Savior's* enterprize." He says, that he
is extremely at a loss to reconcile this proposition with the following texts and many
others, 1 John iii. 8. *For this purpose the*
Son

Son of God was manifested, that he might destroy the works of the devil, and ver. 5. *he was manifested to take away our sins,* and 1 Peter ii. 24. *Christ his ownself bare our sins in his own body on the tree, that we being dead to sin should live unto righteousness,* and Titus ii. 11. 12. *The grace of God which bringeth salvation to all men, hath appeared, teaching us, that denying ungodliness and worldly lusts, we should live soberly, righteously, and godly in this present world,* and ver. 14. *Christ gave himself for us, that he might redeem us from all iniquity, and purify unto himself a peculiar people, zealous of good works.*—Now in assisting him and other readers, who may possibly imagine the like difficulty, to reconcile the aforesaid assertion with these texts and many others to the like purpose; I would ask him the following plain questions: Which should be thought the greater object of view in our Savior's mind, the propagation of his religion in this world, or the establishment of his everlasting kingdom in another?—

and

and whether any reformation which he has effected, or ever will effect in this world, be of equal importance in itself, or equally beneficial to mankind, as that new establishment of things, which we believe will take place by his agency and direction in a future state?—The prevention of vice and the promotion of virtue and piety in any degree that the state of this world admits, can be but preparatory *means,* in order to the compleat abolition of vice, and the establishment of virtue and piety in another world: and these *means* must necessarily be always imperfect, in proportion to the imperfection of the present nature and state of mankind. But were the *means* ever so great and extensive, the *end* must still be greater. The only question then remaining is, Whether the New Testament hath not represented the kingdom of our Savior in another world, and the establishment of things in it, as the principal end of his enterprize—a more important end than any change which will ever

ever be produced in this world by any means whatsoever?—For this I appeal to the whole New Testament: from the whole of which it appears to me, that *that great salvation,* and *that kingdom of God,* which was designed and prepared from the foundation of the world (as a main part of the plan of divine wisdom and goodness in the formation of mankind) for all good men, whether *Christians* or not, are represented as the principal object of our Savior's view and design.—Let us review the foregoing texts, and see their consistency with this supposition. *For this purpose the Son of God was manifested, that he might destroy the works of the devil—and to take away our sins.* And will he not destroy those works, and take away our sins, more perfectly in another world than in this?—*He bare our sins on the cross, that we being dead to sin should live unto righteousness.* And do we not hope to be more dead to sin, and to live more unto righteousness, in a future state than in this?—*The grace of God* undoubtedly *teacheth*

eth us to live soberly, righteously, and godly in this present world—and *Christ gave himself for us,* without doubt, *that he might redeem us from all iniquity, and purify unto himself a peculiar people zealous of good works.* The prevention of iniquity and the promotion of virtue and piety among such as would receive the gospel in the love of it, is, without question, one end and design of our Savior's enterprize, and the principal end for which the gospel was published in the world. But we are witnesses, in how imperfect a degree this end hath taken place: and had it taken place in a far higher degree, we should still consider it only as an *imperfect mean* or preparation, in order to a perfect accomplishment of the like *end* in a future state, where good men will be thorowly redeemed from all iniquity, and zealous of all good works.— It seems as if Mr. *Mason* could not distinguish between the main end of our *Savior's* enterprize, and the main end for which the gospel was published.

I have

I have said, Advert. p. 30. "That there is no such expression to be found in any of the writers of the New Testament, as a resurrection of the body or of the flesh." It seems I am not singular in that opinion. The author of a late celebrated performance (History of Ap. Cr. p. 399.) has said the same thing. In opposition to this opinion, Mr. *Mason* has produced the following passages of Scripture. 1 Cor. xv. 53. *This corruptible must put on incorruption, and this mortal must put on immortality*, and ver. 44. *It is sown a natural body, it is raised a spiritual body.* Now if these expressions can be thought to determine the point; they seem to be more in favor of the supposition, that the *corruptible* and *incorruptible*, the *mortal* and the *immortal*, the *natural* and the *spiritual body*, are not the same, than that they are. But as these expressions may not be thought (to use Mr. *Mason's* terms) sufficiently strong in favor of either supposition; I shall proceed immediately to the other passage, in which

which the apoſtle aſſerts (as he ſays) in the moſt plain and abſolute terms that can be, what I deny. Rom. viii. 11. *If the ſpirit of him that raiſed up Jeſus from the dead dwell in you; he that raiſed up Chriſt from the dead* (ζωοποιησει και τα θνητα σωματα υμων) *ſhall quicken your mortal bodies.* Now in order to ſerve his own purpoſe, and make this text ſeem a direct contradiction to my aſſertion, he hath miſtranſlated it thus, *ſhall make your dead bodies live*—*dead* bodies, as if he did not know the different ſenſe of θνητα and νεκρα, *mortal* and *dead*. The word here is properly rendered in our Engliſh tranſlation *mortal:* and in another paſſage, this *mortal* muſt put on immortality. Is a corpſe, or dead carcaſe, *mortal?* Mr. *Maſon* himſelf is now, I hope, one of των θνητων τετων *theſe mortals* who ſhall put on immortality. But it certainly does not follow from hence that he is νεκρον dead. I hope alſo, that *the ſpirit of him who raiſed up Jeſus from the dead, does now dwell in him,* and does now *quicken* or animate

animate or enliven his *mortal body*, and incite it to the discharge of the spiritual functions of his office, and to every Christian duty. This construction of the words is, I apprehend, agreeable to the true sense of the apostle, and that they have no reference at all to the resurrection. To be convinced of this, let us examine the context; in which the apostle is considering the opposite nature and tendency of a worldly and sensual, to that of a moral and spiritual life: One he stiles, *being in the flesh,—living according to the flesh—and minding the things of the flesh:* the other, *living according to the spirit,* and *minding the things of that:*—and, " they that are in " the flesh," ver. 8. or are governed by it, " cannot please God." *But ye are not in the flesh, but in the spirit, if the spirit of God dwells in you: and, if any man hath not the spirit of Christ, he is none of his. And, if Christ be in you, the body is dead* (already dead, *i. e.* mortified or subdued) *on the account of sin; but the spirit is alive on account*

of

APPENDIX.

of *righteousness. And if the spirit of him that raised up Jesus from the dead dwells in you; he that raised Christ from the dead will* animate or enliven your *mortal bodies by his spirit which dwelleth in you;* and hereby, notwithstanding the weakness and encumbrance of the *flesh,* make them subservient to the dispositions or intentions of the *mind* or *spirit,* in a spiritual and divine life. From whence he concludes, that we are *not debtors to the flesh, to live according to that, but to the spirit.*—If this be the right construction of the passage; it is plain, that it hath no reference at all to the resurrection. And indeed, the supposition, that the flesh shall not be raised again, but the spirit alone live for ever in a new kind of body or habitation, is a better premise than the other supposition of a resurrection of the flesh or of the same body, from which to draw the *apostle*'s inference, that we are *not debtors to the flesh to live according to that, but to the spirit.* However, this question seems, in my apprehension, prehenfion, to be fully decided by the apoftle himfelf, 1 Cor. xv. 35. where he begins profeffedly to explain his notion of a refurrection. *But fome one will fay, How are the dead raifed; and with what body do they come?* that is, (if I underftand the queftion aright) do they come with the fame body, or with one of another kind? To this the *apoftle* replies, *Fool*, (to fuppofe that they come with the fame body) *that which thou foweft is not that body which fhall be, but bare grain—and God giveth it a body as it hath pleafed him.* As then the ftem, leaf, and ear, or in a word, the plant is not the fame with the feed which was fown; much lefs will the future incorruptible, immortal, fpiritual body, be the fame with this corruptible, mortal, animal body. And indeed, is it not *foolifh* to imagine, that our Savior's glorious body is now compounded of the very fame materials, the fame flefh, or blood, or bones, or nerves, or animal fpirits, as that body in which he appeared to his difciples, was feen and handled by them,

them, and visibly ascended to heaven, and in which it was necessary for him to appear, in order to be known?——After all, it is a question of no great moment, as affecting the cause of true piety and the practice of morality; which, as Mr. *Mason* justly observes, is the main scope of the *Christian* institution, and to which all doctrines should be subservient. The chief reason I had for saying so much on this subject, was a hope I conceived of rendering the language of the *New Testament* more intelligible; and of shewing, that the doctrine of a *resurrection*, as it lies in the *New Testament*, is free from those physical difficulties and objections, which arise from the perpetual change of our present bodies, and the dispersion of the materials which compose them into other bodies. Certainly, the divine power stands in no need of such materials, in order to give us hereafter such bodies as it hath pleased him.——I can remind Mr. *Mason* of another text, which he has omitted, and which seems

seems as much to his purpose as those he has quoted. Philip. iii. 21. *Who shall change our vile body, that it may be fashioned like unto his glorious body.* But perhaps he was aware, that this is no more than an allusion to the changes of raiment customary amongst the ancients: as if the *apostle* had said, Who shall strip us of these vile garments, and put on us a habit of raiment of a nobler texture and fashion, even similar to that of *Christ* himself. The *apostle* represents the same change, 2 Cor. v. 1. *For we know that when our earthly tabernacle is dissolved, we have a building from God, a house not made with hands, eternal in the heavens. For in this we groan, desiring to put on,* to take possession of, *our habitation which is from heaven.*

It is hardly worth while to take notice of another remark of his, in which he says, that I define a miracle to be in other words, " a manifest effect and de-
" monstration of the power and providence
" of

" of God:" which he says " makes every
" thing we see to be a miracle." And it is
very true, that every thing we see is a miracle; and has been said to be so by better
writers than myself. This is only using
the word in a *general* sense; and I have
in the very same paragraph distinguished
that *general* sense from the *particular* and
strict sense in which the word miracle is
commonly used. Thus:—" there are per-
" petually occurring to us in the natural
" course of things, numberless events as
" truly miraculous, as those which from
" their rarity and singularity have obtain-
" ed, in a more strict sense, the name of
" miracles. That the sun or the earth
" moves continually, is as truly marvellous,
" as if we suppose the motion was once
" suspended. The formation of every in-
" fant in the womb, is as wonderful an
" effect, and argues divine power and wis-
" dom as much as the original formation
" of *Adam* from the dust of the earth."—
Here it is plain, that I use the term *miraculous*

culous in a *general* fenfe, and in the fame fenfe as the terms *marvellous* and wonderful, or arguing divine power and wifdom. If he had quoted the paffage *fairly*, the reader would have feen, that I did not intend to give a definition of a miracle.

As to my faying, that "the title of "*Chrift*'s vicar or fubftitute on earth, *ex-* "*actly* anfwers to the word *antichrift*;" if he will only add, what is eafily underftood, *Chrift*'s pretended vicar or fubftitute, but real adverfary; I will then defire him to do, what he ought to have done, give a *more exact* definition, or elfe fuffer this to pafs.

Having gone through this gentleman's remarks on my writings, I can affure him, that I think his writings contain many good fentiments of piety and morality; and that I fhould think it an office *very unworthy of myfelf*, to ranfack them, in order to pick out and expofe to view weak and

and exceptionable paſſages. But he has not thought the ſame office *unworthy of himſelf* in reſpect to mine. With what ſucceſs he has attempted this, let thoſe judge who chuſe to examine: or to uſe a modern phraſe, let the world judge, that *little world* to which his writings and mine may chance to be known.

I am ſorry that he is ready to ſuppoſe, that by the term *blind believers* I meant himſelf and his friends; which I could not do, as I had no acquaintance with any of them, nor knew what his opinions were, having read only ſome of his practical works. His words are, " A " writer of this complexion will imme-" diately pronounce *us* blind believers." But why the term *us?* Are there not blind believers enow in the church of *Rome*, and in all proteſtant churches; who in Mr. *Maſon*'s own opinion, defend ſome doctrines as fundamental to *Chriſtianity*, which are either injurious to the cauſe of it, or no way

way belong to it, or are obscure and doubtful? Why then must he needs fill up the number with himself and his friends?

However, this same gentleman, who appears so exceedingly sensible of any reflexion (though not intended) upon his *opinions*, yet does not scruple to begin a direct attack upon my *qualifications* as an author, and to throw out *personal* invectives. For in describing my complexion as a writer, his terms are, "Who strips
" Christianity of its most essential excel-
" lences—inadvertently disfigures the re-
" ligion he means to defend—pares off its
" superfluities with too hasty a hand, and
" wounds it to the quick——by crowding
" too much sail when the ballast is light,
" he is in danger of running upon the
" shelves, and of making shipwreck of his
" faith, judgment, and charity——he is
" incapable of self-diffidence—has not the
" least compassion to men's prejudices—
" and is entirely unconscious that he stands
" in

" in any need of that candor which he
" denies to others——he difcovers fuch
" marks of temerity and precipitance, as
" will be of no advantage to him in mak-
" ing profelytes——In fhort, he is lopping
" off the main branches of *Chriftianity*."

This is fuch language as every author may expect to meet with, who expreffes his fentiments, *nec temere, nec timide*, with a freedom and perfpicuity that befpeaks an honeft mind, whenever they happen to clafh with certain received opinions. All that I learn from it is this, that Mr. *Mafon* is very much difpleafed, that I have the prefumption to differ from him and others, in explaining the New Teftament, and to deny fome metaphyfical notions of his, which he looks upon as effential branches of *Chriftianity*, to be any doctrines of *Chriftianity* at all. I readily confefs, that I believe, the compofition of feveral perfons in one fubftance, or the analyfion of one fubftance into feveral perfons, to be no more

more a doctrine of *Christianity*, than the transubstantiation of the elements of bread and wine into the very body, soul, and divinity of our *Savior*. If we should allow such chemical or physical or metaphysical notions to be possible in the nature of things, it does by no means follow, that they are *Christian* doctrines.

It is pleasant to observe the same gentleman, who has complimented me with such language, pleading for candor, and declaring, that he did not " *intend to give* " *the least offence to the ingenious author,*" with whom he takes this freedom.

What his motive was for attacking me in this manner, I do not pretend to determine; but by way of conjecture would recommend to him the following lines of *Hesiod*:

Καὶ κεραμευς κεραμει κοτεει, καὶ τεκτονι τεκτων,
Καὶ πτωχο· πτωχω φθονεει, καὶ αοιδο· αοιδω.

F I N I S.

www.ingramcontent.com/pod-product-compliance
Lightning Source LLC
Chambersburg PA
CBHW022103300426
44117CB00007B/567